THE GIFT *of* GRIEF

Grief is not an end in itself. It's something you have to live with and walk through.

CLIVE E. NEIL

FOREWORD BY BRYAN STEVENSON, EJI

The Gift of Grief

This book is not intended as a guide to diagnose or treat medical or psychological problems. If you require medical, psychological, or other expert assistance, please seek the services of a physician or mental health professional.

Scriptures taken from *The Holy Bible, King James Version*. Cambridge Edition: 1769; *King James Bible Online*, 2025. www.kingjamesbibleonline.org.

Library of Congress Control Number: 2026903948

Paperback ISBN: 978-1-966283-27-0
Hardcover ISBN: 978-1-969063-95-4

1. Main category—RELIGION / Christian Living / Death, Grief, Bereavement
2. Other category—SELF-HELP / Death, Grief, Bereavement
3. Other category—RELIGION / Christian Living / Personal Memoirs

Published by American Real Publishing
Binghamton, NY
americanrealpublishing.com

TABLE OF CONTENTS

DEDICATION

To my beloved mom and dad,

Though you are no longer here in the body, your spirit lives in every step I take.

Your unwavering commitment to discipline, sacrifice, and hard work laid the foundation of my character. You taught me the value of showing up, of doing my best even when no one is watching, and believing that purpose is greater than comfort.

Your lives were not easy, but you never let hardship steal your dignity or determination.

Because of you, I strive to live with integrity. Because of you, I am who I am today.

This book is a tribute to your legacy, your love, your grace, and your teaching—principles that are forever etched in the fiber of my soul and lived out in every lesson I pass forward.

Thank you for everything.

I love you always.

FOREWORD

If we love, we will, at times, unquestionably have to grieve. There are libraries filled with books, poetry, and scholarship on the power of love, but comparatively little on grief. As an attorney and advocate for the poor, I have stood next to condemned prisoners, people abused and abandoned, mothers and fathers who suffer with heartbreaking loss, young people devastated by tragedy and trauma. I know that grief is one of the most powerful forces shaping human behavior. In courtrooms, community rooms, and cramped holding cells. I have seen how unresolved sorrow can turn into anger, isolation, poor decision-making, and cycles of pain that pass from one generation to the next. Emotional distress when left unacknowledged becomes a silent architect of lives undone. How people see themselves, how they relate to others, and how they respond to life's pressures can't be understood without some attention to the grief they carry.

Clive Neil offers us something helpful and valuable in this thoughtful new work. I've known my former college roommate for decades, and he has the kind of intellectual curiosity and rigor to offer an important, detailed examination of something we will all face. Importantly, Clive's work educates readers on what grief actually is: a complex psychological, emotional, and even physical experience that must be understood, not feared. The educational value of this book cannot be overstated. It equips readers with knowledge that schools rarely teach and society rarely acknowledges. It unpacks the stages, patterns, and expressions of grief in ways that help readers identify what they are feeling and why. More importantly, it teaches practical strategies for moving through pain rather than being controlled by it.

In expanding our understanding of grief, this book becomes a kind of emotional curriculum—one that strengthens the mind while soothing the heart. Readers will learn how grief affects decision-making, mental health, relationships, and even the ability to succeed academically or professionally. For families, clergy, counselors, teachers, community leaders, and anyone working with vulnerable populations, this book serves as a resource that can change not just individual lives but entire communities.

We live in a world that struggles to be empathetic toward others. For healthier families, communities, and relationships, we must become better educated and equipped to understand others' challenges. *Rugged Terrain* offers deep compassion for all who have been wounded. It validates the quiet fears, the internal battles, and the feelings of being overwhelmed or misunderstood. This book teaches us that grief is not weakness and healing is not linear. By addressing these truths with empathy and clarity, we are taught to feel, to reflect, and to rebuild.

Clive Neil has always met people where they are and this book is no exception. He has an uncanny gift for feeding our mind with detailed research and insight and calming our heart with kindness and compassion. Clive teaches without judging, guides without pushing. Whether someone is grieving a loved one, a relationship, a dream, or a part of themselves they feel they have lost, this book helps them understand their journey and offers hope where despair once lived.

At a time when there is so much fear, anger and division in the world, we see unacknowledged grief manifesting in so many destructive and unhealthy ways. We need this book. It is more than a guide—it is a lifeline that will give readers the tools to understand their own emotions, support others in their pain, and break cycles of silent suffering. I believe it will inspire healthier individuals, stronger families, and more compassionate communities.

May the wisdom found in these pages transform your understanding of grief and empower you to heal, grow, and find renewed purpose.

Bryan Stevenson

Equal Justice Initiative, Director

Montgomery, Alabama

INTRODUCTION

At first, everything feels surreal. Time freezes. I may hear the words, but my mind refuses to accept them. It's as if the world suddenly changed its rules without warning. The breath is knocked out of me, and nothing feels real. There is a physical ache in my chest, like something heavy is sitting on my soul. A deep, hollow pain that won't go away—because it comes from love ripped away too soon. The one who carried me, nurtured me, prayed over me, is gone—and that truth breaks something sacred inside of me. I'm overwhelmed with a desperate, aching need to hear her voice one more time...to feel her hand, to smell her familiar scent, to say the things I didn't get to say.

Every memory is a trigger. Every silence is too loud. I find myself reaching for the phone, forgetting...then remembering. I may feel anger at life, at God, at the unfairness of it all. Why now? Why like this? Why her? These questions haunt the mind because there are no satisfying answers, only pain that has nowhere to go. There's a void that nothing fills. A sense that the world has lost its color. Its warmth, its balance. Her absence feels like a shadow that follows me into every room. I replay moments, wondering if I said enough, did enough, showed enough love. I may question myself, though I did my best. This grief carries whispers of "what if," even when it's undeserved.

Grief is a word we all know how to spell, but we can never truly know it until it becomes our personal reality. For me, grief isn't something that comes over me like a little wave of sadness. It's a companion that never goes away. I've learned that grief is a type of prayer. It's wordless, raw, and achingly honest. And it is in these thresholds that I have experienced both the depths of loss and the surprising presence of the Divine, sometimes even at the same time.

It arrived uninvited, lodging itself in my chest and my head, and reshaping my world after I'd lost my mom, my dad, and two of my brothers. My life became a fragmented story without their presence, each chapter incomplete, each page saturated with the pain of longing. The pain is constant. Some days, it's a jagged reminder of everything I've lost that steals my breath. Other days it's quieter but no less heavy. Rather, a dull ache that feels like it's infiltrating every last corner of my being lingers without reprieve. It's the empty chair at the table, the quiet where laughter used to resound, the pictures that seem stuck in a world I can never go back to.

I felt like losing my parents, in a way, was like losing the roots that held me. These were my history, my signposts, my sanctuary. Without them, the world feels unmoored, like I was wandering around in a storm with no place to connect to. For over thirty-five years I have walked with people into the deepest valleys of their lives, offering, to the best of my ability, comfort and care as they have struggled to deal with loss in all its forms. I have sat with mothers who have buried children, with children who have buried parents, with marriages that have died a slow death, with dreams that have been laid to rest, yet losing my own felt like it was the first time.

We talk about grief as if it were a one-size-fits-all phenomenon, a uniform experience of sorrow with easily identifiable stages and a culturally acceptable timeline. But grief is not singular. It's a whole series of events, plural, complex, and highly individual, with no timeline or order. The grief that comes after death has its own gravity, its own customs, its own acknowledgment by the world around us. This is the kind of grief people send flowers for. They bring cakes and pies. They know to say, "How are you holding up?" But what about the grief that has no funeral, no obituary, no social frame to contain it? How about grieving for the person you once were, the dreams you once thought would come true, the identity that used to fit so easily, like a second skin, but now hangs off you, alien and unfamiliar?

Once I lost my voice, I went into a grief cycle that was new for me. It sent me into this spiral of pain that, for a moment, I worried I wouldn't be able to come back from. The short-term grieving process overwhelmed me and resulted in daily mental and emotional scabbing over. But it also changed the way I think of mourning and loss and what grief is meant to do to our lives. The body bears all these griefs. It has the phantom weight of arms that will never wrap around you again, the muscle memory of gestures that you once shared with people who have left. But it also holds the echo of who you used to be. Whether it's the way you once held yourself with the posture of confidence strong enough to command the room, the fast and free laugh that fell so naturally from your lips, or the way you simply came to walk through the world when you believed different things about yourself, about life, about what you were even capable of, grief takes you and changes you.

My great lesson of sorrow is this: Sorrow brings with it renewal and renovation. Grief not only breaks our heart, but it also breaks our brain, severing the cognitive functions that help us make sense of loss, and allows us to cling to God in a way we never have before. Sadness doesn't take your joy. It helps you find more purpose in it. These emotions are not signs of weakness. They're evidence of the love, bond, and history I shared. Grief this deep only exists where love once lived deeply.

The aching loss of my loved ones is something I bear with me daily. It's a black hole that nothing, neither time nor distraction, can ever really fill. And yet, in that unbearable ache, I've come to realize that grief also made something of me. It fostered the faith to endure, the courage to feel, and somehow, the strength to carry on.

This book grew out of an acknowledgment of these grieving moments. The grief of death and the grief of transformation are not two separate experiences, but two threads in the same human tapestry of loss. This book is my effort to speak of that pain, process that pain, and rise from the pain. An attempt to establish some of what it means to live with grief, which is endless, but is also grounded in love.

There are nights I have cried myself to sleep. That is not something I am ashamed of, rather, it is a reality of my truth. There are days I threw myself into work or ministry to avoid facing the reality of loss. But there are also moments of clarity when the memories push through the darkness and create delicate, halting steps into something that shaped my healing.

The prophet Isaiah tells us that God gives beauty for ashes, joy for mourning, a garment of praise for a heaviness of spirit. But this divine exchange is not magic that makes our pain go away. The process is a slow, sacred one of learning to carry both sorrow and hope, both absence and presence, both the truth of where you have lost, and the promise of what God is still doing in and through us.

To everyone who's felt that same unbearable weight, this is for you. You are not walking this path alone. Together, perhaps you and I can find a way to bear our sorrow—not only to bear it, but to bear witness to the love that is left. It is not whether or not you will be changed by what you lose, but who you will become from it. The question is not whether you will learn to live with grief but how you will learn to live from it.

This is not a book about getting through grief or over it. It's a book about carrying on with it, learning to carry multiple losses at once, and learning that the heart is bigger than you thought. The heart is large enough to contain the presence of love and the absence of love, large enough to contain the people you have lost and the people you have been. I propose that maybe our losses might address one another, and the capacities we develop in grieving our dead may assist us in freeing our past selves.

I welcome you to the pages that follow, where I invite readers into an exploration of these questions with me. To sit with the complexity of loss, to honor the myriad ways it lives within us, and to know that in naming our losses, we do not become diminished. Instead, we create room for everything we have been, everything we are, and everything we've yet to become.

CHAPTER 1

THE PURPOSE OF GRIEF

Grief is a paradox. It feels like destruction, anger, sadness, imperfection, hurt, relief, truth, and solitude all in one. Raging like the winds and floods of a Category 5 hurricane, leaving nothing but unrest in its path. Tearing through the heart, leaving it shattered and raw without direction of who to blame. It's an unraveling.

Yet, buried within that destruction lies the seed of an undescribed transformation waiting to unfold. In the unbearable pain of loss, there exists a strange and profound purpose. The purpose of grief is to help individuals emotionally and psychologically process the impact of loss. Though it may take us months, years, or even a lifetime to recognize it, there is a purpose to grief. Grief is not a punishment, nor is it an obstacle to overcome. It is a passage, one that reshapes you as you learn to live with the weight of love's absence.

I remember that day like it was yesterday.

It was a regular day in March—March 8, 2015, to be exact. I had gotten up, done my devotional, and prepared for another Sunday. I left home and headed to Brooklyn in my car. The phone call came at 7:16 a.m., right as I turned the corner of Nostrand Avenue and Fulton Street. The ring of a phone that I'd heard many times before, the road I was all too familiar with driving, became the scene of a heartbreak I had never known before. As the initial words came through the phone, I was unable to accept that they were true. My body was rigid, unable to bend, my mind racing and questioning everything that I knew and held dear, my soul shattered to pieces, and I was unable to comprehend how I would ever be able to put the pieces back together.

It was my brother-in-law Dennis (now deceased) on the other end of the phone, his voice a faint whisper that barely registered over the pounding in my ears. "Clive, it's Mom… She's gone."

The words hung in the air, suspended from the abyss of disbelief. Gone. A word so small, too inadequate to encompass the heaviness of the fracture that had just forever altered my world. A word too minute to encompass where she had gone spiritually, it still carried the unacceptable fact that she was no longer here in the physical realm. My mother. The person who kept me grounded, the moral compass of our family, the prayer warrior, the only person who knew me from conception until now, was gone. It felt surreal, a lie, a nonfiction novel I no longer had interest in reading. And without control, prompt, or approval, the flood of tears began to fall. I could no longer see straight or hear anything from the busy street that was around me. My world as I understood it was no more.

The next few hours played out in a blur of fragmented instances and actions performed on autopilot. I was out of control. Not reckless, but mindless, heartless, thoughtless. The raw shock numbed every sense in my body, reducing me to a shell. Hollow in making, void in nature, I arrived at the church, greeted congregants, and tried to navigate the morning as I did almost every other Sunday. I was offering a constant stream of prayers that I could keep it all together, but when we stepped into prayer, I broke. How could I pray for others when I felt nothing? Where else could I lay the weight of what happened other than at the feet of the Lord? To say I recall the details would be untrue. My body moved, words formed, but I was truly not in control. The practical tasks, notifying family, arranging the funeral, still pastoring while grieving, were accomplished through a haze of emotional detachment. Each phone call, each whispered condolence, felt like a distant echo in a world that had already begun to dissolve around me.

My mom was gone. To be honest, I did what I knew best. I stayed busy, I nodded, said thank you for the condolences, and proceeded to do the work.

As I made arrangements for the service and for my family, it became routine to push feelings to the back of my mind and press forward. It wasn't until the time had come for me to head to Jamaica for the service that the subscription to my denial membership ran out. I had some time, a moment to be still, and thought it was the opportune moment to prepare a tribute to my mother. What could I say that would capture all she meant to me? What could I say to my sisters that would provide comfort for them and assure them that she was now at peace and rejoicing in Heaven with the Lord? My eyes began to flood with tears, and my hand began to tremble, too unsteady to scribe any words, so instead, I shut my eyes and pleaded with God that this would somehow be untrue.

Through the planning, calling, and arranging, I threw myself into the day-to-day aspects of life in hopes of numbing the pain that riddled my body. But I could no longer ignore what stood before me. Holding it in only piled on, and I could no longer deny the weight in my chest. It was in those agonizing moments, surrounded by the tangible presence of grief, that I began to touch the iceberg containing the depth and complexity of processing what had happened to me. This wasn't simply sadness. It was a complete and utter unraveling, a shattering of my very core. The ground beneath my feet crumbled, leaving me adrift in a sea of sorrow, with no compass, no map, and no clear sense of direction.

The mental cost of grief is more expansive than we know, as it captures our ability to concentrate, to decide things, to think, and even to continue thinking. In the months after my losses, I began to stand in my kitchen, forgetting why I had walked into it. I'd be in the middle of sentences, and my thoughts would evaporate while I was speaking. My reading, my one lasting comfort, had slowed down and even stopped. The words on the pages lacked sense, lacked meaning.

Even sleep was a battlefield, a struggle of tossing and turning. Every night would bring the plunge into a restless ocean of nightmares and jumbled recollections. The contrast of agony and joy in my memories made me crumble into a ball again and yearn for the touch of comfort. Praying felt smothered in the anguish of her loss. I would simply hear her singing, her words echoing in my mind as I attempted to pray. It would disappear in a waterfall of hyper-mental suffering, as if nothing was safe from the reach of my pain, not even my own thoughts.

When thinking of the unraveling experience of grieving, I began to travel through the physical, mental, and emotional stages. They all impacted my body differently. I had considered grief, imagined the hollow emptiness of her no longer being around, but the physicality caught me off guard. The physical stuff hit me hard, unexpectedly, overwhelming. Headaches, stomachaches, and weakened immune systems are not uncommon as the signatures of grief. Yet they happened to me in waves, sometimes planned, most times unplanned, all while still settling in my being. This physical pain compounded the already intolerable burden of grief. This was a total physical collapse, a testament to the body's deep response to loss. I was tired, paralyzingly so, and my body was slack with unreasoned tears and unvoiced grief.

Food brought no solace, as I had no appetite. Each meal was an effort, a memory of the happiness and culture we had both cherished in the kitchen. The burning, constant pain in my chest turned out to be a physical representation of my emotional pain but also served as a cruel reminder of my loss. I lost weight, my mind was a million miles away, and I would cry at the oddest times. There was no way of stopping the constant sadness that washed over me, almost drowning me in my grief. Even the easiest tasks, things that had been easy as biscuits, required a mental effort that I did not have to give and left me feeling mentally, emotionally, and physically drained and shot through.

As I write this now, I have had the opportunity to discuss this with other grievers, welcoming their take on what happens to our brains as we grieve. The conclusion has been that our brain undergoes a matter of rewiring when we are grieving. The fog that settles over us is not a character flaw but a biological response, the way the brain protects itself, keeping us from taking in more information than it can handle, while it does the massive work of rebounding from the absence of someone central to our world.

After one very long evening of sitting in my study, unable to concentrate on the sermon I knew I had to write, surrounded by tissues with no end in sight, I was asking the question, what in the world was the point of all of this? What good could come out of this feeling that everything in my being is completely torn apart, body, mind, and soul? Why, if God is really loving and close to us in our suffering, would He be encouraging people to be such a catastrophe of frailty in the light of suffering? The questions seemed a combination of disrespectful and irrelevant, the sort of blunt murmurings of Job or the pained cry of the psalmists. I started to think that maybe grief was not only a cruel accident of evolution, but also a bug in our system, a malfunction that made us suffer more than was necessary.

What the body does in grief illustrates the mind-body connection in a clear way, showing how the pain of the heart can have physical consequences. It's an important thing to acknowledge that our bodies are thirsty for that rest and nourishment and care during this challenging time, where we're all trying to figure out a way through a type of darkness. To refuse to be 'bowed to your bent' in bodily cares of sorrow is only to bring this burden more heavily upon the mind.

I said to God, "Why is this agony so deep? What can I use as my motivation for life now that she's gone?" I was caught up in trying to figure out this stranger who had been created by an unforeseen villain, a stranger I could neither escape nor had any interest in getting to know. I felt like the home and stability I once enjoyed, centered around my family and Mom's nurturing warmth, had been ripped out from under me. The world was alien, and so was I, searching for meaning and solace in a hurt that's unimaginable to anyone else on Earth.

The unsettling nature of grief is that you have to allow yourself to unravel before you can even begin the process. There is this sense of powerlessness that has to occur before understanding what it means to not be okay. Every mental, emotional, psychological thing experienced as a result of grieving is normal. It may not have been mentioned in a book or noted as an assured thing to experience as a result, but everyone grieves differently, and every feeling is valid.

It felt as if I had been ripped from limb to limb, leaving an irreplaceable hole where my unity and contentment once dwelled. And because of this, I was certain no one would understand what I was going through. My pain was personal, it cut deep, and I did not desire fleeting condolences.

The manner in which my body let go of this pain, physiologically, cognitively, and emotionally, illustrated that inasmuch as you love people in life, you must grieve for them. At base, grief is a sign of the depth of our connection. It is the measure of our love, the gauge of a life well-lived, someone well-loved.

This action of mourning and unraveling is seen also when we mourn aspects of our lives that are not tied to physical people. Losing an element of yourself hurts just as much, but that is often refined to something that you should just get over because it "could be worse." When we mourn, we pay homage to those connections, even as we grapple with the pain of their disappearance. It does force us to remember our own fragility and the gift that each day holds. It wakes us up to the ephemeral beauty of what we were once taking for granted.

Questions for Thought:

In your life, what have you grieved or are grieving?

Who have you grieved or are grieving?

What are your memories of unraveling?

Do you feel like you have unraveled post grief?

One Step at a Time—From Why to How

The song writer says: "One day at a time, sweet Jesus, that's all I am asking of you. Lord, give me the strength to do everything that I have to do." I can be honest that my early attempts at coping were clumsy. More like surface-level attempts to dress a gaping wound with a Band-Aid. I failed to understand why I was experiencing this level of void, but also why I had no control over what it was doing to my body. I had buried many people before, "ashes to ashes, dust to dust," yet here I was unable to move forward. I found myself seeking solace in solitude, hoping that if I retreated from the world, I would somehow get through the pain faster, while hiding from the cliché things that only worsened my pain. I was trying to pass on the entire grief process, as opposed to looking at it as something I would need to overcome one day at a time.

Grief is a deeply personal journey, an environment as layered and varied as me or you. It's not a uniform experience, neatly packaged and easily defined, but it is one that holds similar threads that make the experience recognizable. To begin understanding the purpose of grief, we must move beyond surface-level understanding, as if it's just sadness and loss. We have to acknowledge it as a diverse collection of emotional, physical, psychological, and social dimensions. Being honest with the weight we're experiencing, and how this weight makes us feel, is the only way we are able to make strides toward coping.

As I review my initial feelings, I would like to say that I became a functional griever. Present where I needed to be, engaged with the people who needed me, but yet still yearning on the inside. I knew something was missing, but the "something" couldn't come back, so what would I use to fix it? Friends and family offered their support, but their attempts fell short of understanding where I was and what I was thinking. How could "my condolences" or "I know what you are going through" be a solution to my pain? They just sounded like empty attempts at sounding empathetic.

The expectation of maintaining outward appearances, of putting on a brave face, added to the burden. The façade of normalcy was a mask I wore, concealing the raw, visceral pain that lurked beneath the surface. It was an act of survival, a desperate attempt to navigate a world that seemed intent on ignoring my grief, a world that demanded resilience despite my utter exhaustion and emotional fragility. What I was experiencing was not weakness but the body's natural response to profound loss. Our bodies are systems designed to slow us down, to force us to reckon with what we have lost rather than rushing past it. But if we are not comfortable, we can fall into the trap of trying to defy this, and instead, dive into the deep end to avoid facing the facts.

With time, moments with God and quiet reflection brought peace. It is there I was able to cling to a hope that I felt was so far distanced in the beginning. It was the ability not to overcome grief but to take steps in the way of grieving. Dr. Mary-Frances O'Conner mentions in her book, *The Grieving Brain: The Surprising Science of How We Learn from Love and Loss*, that there is a difference between grief and grieving.[1] She mentioned that grief is a feeling one has, an intense wave of emotion that overwhelms you. Grieving, on the other hand, is how grief changes over time without ever actually going away. It's how you learn to manage and cope with the loss as a new and integral part of you, rather than just a momentary nuisance you have to get over. With this newfound knowledge, I no longer held myself to the expectation that I had to get over grief and began to understand I would need to go along with grieving. I was doing myself a disservice, and in some ways even holding myself back, by feeling that I was taking too long, or taking up too much space. I was hindering my relationship with God by not bringing my feelings to Him. I was hoping He would just know without my saying it in prayer, without my calling out to Him. But releasing it through my mouth, with my groans, and through my tears, was a part of the process. I had to put worth to truth, and with that truth came power.

"There is a sacredness in tears. They are the messengers of overwhelming grief, of deep contrition, and of unspeakable love."

—Washington Irving

In the quiet moments, amidst the chaos and the pain, glimmers of hope began to emerge. The stillness that had scared me no longer intimidated me. Rather, it gave me a chance to speak to God about how I would move forward. It was a dim light, a sparkle in the darkness, but it was enough to keep me going, to get me through another step. It was enough to start. It would be a long and hard journey with many obstacles and hurdles to overcome. But I somehow just knew, with a calm assurance, that I would navigate these same challenges, however hard, however insurmountable they may appear. I would be guided by the memory of her strength, her courage, and with the hand of God.

---

1 O'Connor, M.-F. (2022). *The grieving brain: The surprising science of how we learn from love and loss*. HarperOne.

In the shared grief with my siblings there was a strange form of solace. In the support of cherished friends there was a sense of connection, of being seen and understood. In the love of my congregation and fellow pastors, there was a sense of love from God himself, one that is limitless yet still encompassing at the same time. These moments, though fragile and fleeting, were crucial, providing a temporary respite from the unrelenting onslaught of sorrow. They served as quiet reminders that while grief was powerful, it didn't have to define me entirely. The initial shock might have shattered my world, but somewhere within the fragments, within the pain and the chaos, lay the potential for rebuilding. The path was uncertain, fraught with challenges. But the faintest glimmer of hope, a persistent ember in the heart of my darkness, ignited a resolve within me. It was the beginning of a long, arduous journey, but it was a journey I was determined to undertake.

At first, I fought the physical aspects of grief. I felt the effort, even if it drained my body. These actions of resistance failed, and in the end, made me worse. The pure stubbornness of denial, of refusing to acknowledge how deeply I hurt, led me to a more overwhelming, more profound place of exhaustion and misery. I was heartbroken, but it was a profound, sorrowful discovery. This was the first thing I encountered for a while that I couldn't just "get over" or "pray away." It was grudging acceptance, a painful but essential leap toward healing.

Embracing my physical and emotional condition for what it was meant accepting the fact that my grief was purposeful in some way. Reviewing past sermons, and the Bible, I found other Bible folk who were transformed by periods of grief. This pain wasn't a character flaw but my brain's natural response to loss. In the same way it changed as I formed these bonds of love, it was now changing as these bonds were being adjusted. I had to admit that I am human and thus feel human emotions. It was one of those moments when self-compassion started to nudge out self-reproach. This admission set the foundation of a kinder, gentler path toward healing and grieving. It wasn't until I acknowledged my body's reaction to grief as normal, that I allowed myself to admit I wasn't abnormal for feeling any of it, that I started to heal.

Although this admission was a tough pill to swallow, it saved me, healing me a little piece at a time. Gradually, I started to feel the quiet shifts. Sleep started to come a little bit easier. The heartbreaking dreams subsided to some degree, only to be replaced by less rattling and more calming themes. My hunger came back, at least tentatively and a little bit gradually. The food provided the opportunity to gain nutrients and think of the fact that I was doing something to take care of me. The tightness in my chest began to loosen, and the continual anxiousness subsided. It was a slow, grueling process, but the tiny little shifts, the baby steps of growth, represented a morsel of hope, an indication that yes, what I thought we could heal, in fact, we could.

To say I knew the dates and times of these healing instances would be a lie. Honestly speaking, they are still happening and taking form in my life. It began to dawn upon me that my body, the material that made me, was learning to find its place in this new world, piecing itself together, slowly, little by little, as it adjusted to life after loss. There was much healing to be done, but the tangible evidence of recovery was an extraordinary comfort and testament to just how resilient the body and spirit can be. The process of grief is not just emotional. It's very physical, and it requires letting go of understanding, acceptance of the unknown, and deep compassion for yourself.

When I consider the intention of grief, the effect it produces upon the body, I am convinced that it is intended to motivate us to surrender control, surrender ourselves to God. Accepting the physical reality of my grief meant accepting that it was okay to take a break, to prioritize sleep, to give myself the time to heal from the emotional and the physical cost. It meant treating my body kindly, feeding it healthy food and encouraging gentle movement, and understanding that post-inpatient treatment would mean working not just on my mind, but my body as well. It was a slow road, a gradual realization that physical and emotional health were deeply linked. I had to move from thinking, "Why is this happening?" to "How is today better than yesterday?"

Grieving is not simply looking backward but a process of coming to terms with the new landscape of our lives. Nothing is the same after a big loss. The routines, the relationships, and the lives we led at one time are permanently changed. Grief is the only way to steer between these deadly relations, even though its hard counsel is intolerable. It requires us to release what once was, despite how tightly our hearts hold onto what's past. In letting go, we also start to create room, a new reality that we didn't choose but have to inhabit all the same. In the throes of grief, there is always that moment the pain is truly too much. It has become like the world has turned to ash, as if anything good, anything worthwhile, can never be again. But it is in this hot crucible of grief that we are slowly and painfully changed. It peels back illusions so that we are forced to reckon with who we are, once the people or things we have lost are gone. It teaches us the virtues of resilience, no matter how much we fight its lessons. It rearranges our priorities and brings to mind what really counts.

Questions for Thought:

What does it mean to accept something I never wanted?

How can I create space for grief to coexist with other emotions?

How do I want to spend my energy when I have so little to spare?

How might I be gentle with myself as I figure out this new normal?

The Point of It All

Looking back, those early coping strategies were a combination of desperation and natural reactions. The truth is, the purpose of grief is never easily digestible. It is tough to sit with, because there is no elegant grief process. There is no guidebook, no manual on how to cross into this uncharted land of how I was feeling. I was at sea, drowning in my grief, clinging to any floaty or jet ski I could get my hands on, trying frantically to keep my head above water. The gestures, though not enough to alleviate my grief, had a function, however minuscule. They shaped the façade of normalcy that allowed me to negotiate the initial chaotic stage of profound loss. What we have are the illusion of ritual, the temporary distraction, the silent presence of family. These were tiny, tender islands of solace in a sea of grief.

The point of grieving is that it enables people to actually recover and emotionally function again, to find new meaning after loss, and then to get on with the job of living a resilient life despite that loss. Healing doesn't erase the past, and healing doesn't mean "moving on" in the sense that others might seek. True healing is about integration. It's about learning how to live with loss inside of us, not as a burden that inhibits us, but as an element of what we are. Grief changes us, without a doubt, but that change fosters growth, renewal, and strength. It can make us more loving, more understanding, more grateful. It can bring us further into our own lives, more in tune with the ephemeral beauty of the world around us.

I was starting to discover something very deep in the act of unraveling. The total breakdown I had suffered was not a glitch in the system, but a rewiring. It was an essential dismantling, an absolutely sacred unbecoming that needed to unfold prior to any kind of actual restoration. Writer and relationship strategizer Katie Rössler, a leading expert in traumatic grief, calls this process "the cocoon stage."[2] As you are cocooning, your thoughts, beliefs, and opinions are changing. It may not feel good, but it is in this space that all the chemical changes are happening to shed this old self in preparation for the new.

The body fatigue had slowed me down and caused me to narrow my focus to only things that really mattered. All that emotional instability had opened my heart up like never before. The haze of my brain had undercut my usual defenses and coping strategies, and I was left exposed to the presence of God in ways I had rarely felt when I was "well."

This perspective revolutionized my attitude toward grief, full stop. It was not something to sit through or soldier through but something to surrender to, a purging that makes space for new growth. Like a forest fire that burns through dead undergrowth to allow space for new life, grief scorches away all that is not absolutely essential, all that cannot withstand the flame of loss. The person I had been before my parents died, had left. What remained dwindled even more when having to bury two brothers and a brother-in-law. This is hard to understand, but it was not because that prior person was

---

2 Rössler, K. (2021). *The New Face of Grief: Transform Pain into Empowerment.* Tellwell Talent.

bad. He simply couldn't carry the weight of this new reality. The unwinding of grief is not disintegration—it is preparation. It is the soul's manner of creating space for a greater ability to love, to experience, to comprehend the sweetness of life and the darkness of dying. As I learned to view my unraveling as sacred, not shameful, I caught a glimpse of the resurrection that always waits on the other side of every little death, the new life that can only spring up when we have the courage to be fully undone by love.

In that way, grief is an extreme case of an ending that's also a beginning. It closes one chapter of our lives, but it also sows the seeds for the next. The pain will never entirely go away, but with time, it morphs. It enters the fabric of our own becoming. It's spun naturally into the story of ourselves. And as we pack it on, we also discover that grief, for all the pain it brings, does work to keep us tethered to the love that endures and to lead us toward becoming something new.

When we suffer significant loss, the issue is not whether we will grieve, but rather how. The question is whether we will let grief do its work, to unravel us, to mold us, to change us. It's not an easy path, but it's the one we must travel. There is a purpose to grief. The purpose is often underneath layers of tears, transition, emotions, and heartache, but there is a purpose. It's the time when one loses it all but gains so much more. The time where a heart breaks, but it allows for a new sense of self and passion to rise like a phoenix from the ashes. It's the time when we are faced with silence, while also hearing the Lord the loudest. The Bible says in Psalm 34:18, "The Lord is nigh unto them that are of a broken heart; and saveth such as be of a contrite spirit." If nothing else, grieving draws us closer to God. It gives us fresh eyes to see Him and gives another opportunity to trust him deeper. And in time, grieving may take us not only to healing, but to an interface with what it means to truly be alive.

"Grief is like the ocean; it comes on waves ebbing and flowing. Sometimes the water is calm, and sometimes it is overwhelming. All we can do is learn to swim."

—Vicki Harrison

Questions for Thought:

How might grief slowly reorganize my understanding of my life?

What if the point isn't in the grief itself but in who I become by allowing it?

CHAPTER 2

UNDERSTANDING THE STAGES OF GRIEF

In her groundbreaking work, Elisabeth Kübler-Ross[3] introduced the world to the five stages of grief. She breaks down the barriers of understanding denial, anger, bargaining, depression, and acceptance, and how they are woven together for one to gain clarity and grow from grief. Her detailed and layered approach fits efficiently, as the American Psychology Association[4] describes grief as an anguish experienced after significant loss.

Through these steps, she shed light to the paradoxical nature of grief. The moments of peace, the fleeting glimpses of acceptance, are not signs of weakness or a lack of love for what is no more. Rather, they are subtle shifts in the emotional landscape, pockets of calm amidst the storm. These moments become anchors, helping to navigate the turbulence with more resilience. Understand that moments of pain, peace, and acceptance are natural and necessary for the healing process.

Coming to terms with those moments was necessary when I had to undergo surgery on my vocal cords. In a matter of weeks, it felt like I went through every stage Kübler-Ross mentions in her book. I came to internal-

3 Kübler-Ross, E., & D. Kessler. (2005). *On Grief and Grieving: Finding the Meaning of Grief Through the Five Stages of Loss*. Scribner.

4 https://www.apa.org/topics/grief

ize that grief is not just about the loss of the physical, but also parts of us that are no more. Whether that be the dissolution of a marriage, the loss of a job, dealing with a diagnosis, or healing after surgery, grieving takes place. I navigated the stages, in no clear order, but as Kübler-Ross mentions, the stages provide a heuristic for patterns of thought, emotions, and behavior common in the setting of terminal illness, which may otherwise seem atypical.

There is a unique pain that comes with losing your voice. Not just the physical voice, but the ability to connect, express, and be understood. After my vocal cord surgery, I faced an unexpected kind of grief: the silence and frustration that consumed me for ten long days. What began as a necessary healing process turned into an emotional battle I hadn't anticipated, filled with frustration, isolation, and an overwhelming sense of loss.

When the doctor confirmed that surgery was necessary, so many questions ran through my mind. Why me? I had always been healthy, I go to the gym, I drink green juice, I don't eat meat, I take my vitamins and have regular checkups, so how did we get here? As he mentioned surgery, I remained hopeful that it wouldn't be necessary, but the Lord had other plans.

The surgery went well, and the doctor explained the recovery process included complete vocal rest for ten days. The instructions were straightforward and simple enough. I understood the medical necessity, and I was willing to do whatever it took to heal. Little did I know that no amount of preparation could have readied me for the emotional toll of what it meant to lose my voice.

On that first day, the silence felt like a novelty. Something that I had forgotten I appreciated. I scribbled notes to communicate, waved my hands to express thanks, and thought, *This isn't so bad.* But by the third day, the notion of what I couldn't do started to sink in. I had gone back to my days of infancy, unable to use words to describe how I felt or what I needed. I pictured vocal rest as singers often partake, where they can whisper or speak softly when necessary. But this was different. I couldn't speak at all. At first, I thought all I needed was to rest my voice without considering the weight it would place on my mind, my emotions, my view on life. Simple tasks like answering the phone or calling out to a friend were suddenly impossible. I couldn't even tell my children that I loved them. I couldn't say the words.

I felt misunderstood. It wasn't just the physical act of speaking that I missed. It was the connection, the intimacy of conversation. I hadn't realized how much of my identity was tied to my voice until it was taken away. I went from thinking it wasn't that bad to being angrier than I could have imagined. I began to question if I would sound the same or have that same depth to my voice post recovery. The "what-ifs" and "I-should-haves" took over my mind and left me questioning everything.

As the days stretched on, I began to see the silence differently, and I began to accept what was happening. This was God's hand in disguise. This period of silence forced me to slow down, to listen in ways I hadn't before. I had an opportunity to draw silence, and be silent, post a time in my life where I was speaking a lot. Although I was uncomfortable, I had to unravel, to be angry, to be depressed, to question, before I could see the purpose of this time. Conversations became more about truly hearing others than preparing my response. I noticed the little things that make conversation meaningful, like the way someone's eyes lit up when they spoke, the pauses in their sentences, the emotions behind their words.

When I first learned about the stages of grief, I can be honest that they just seemed like self-explanatory terms that couldn't fully express what a person was feeling. But as I found myself in this space, most importantly after the loss of family and after having surgery that impacted my voice, I developed a greater respect and appreciation for the stages of grief. I began to see them less as tools to navigate the waters, and more like bus stops that you find yourself encountering, staying a while, leaving, and in some cases returning to. The value of these stages is the freedom of fluidity they provide, as they are not be-all and end-all solutions. Nor are they predefined necessities one must experience to have actually grieved. Rather, they are opportunities to be comforted by knowing you are not alone and there is no start or end, but the opportunity to grow beyond.

Although I had counseled numerous members through their grief and discussed it in learning spaces previously, I never imagined that my own would consume me in the manner it did. Everything I felt was normal, yet so abnormal. With grief, it often feels like the path to feeling and living again is unclear, but the reality is, feeling is only one stage. As we navigate the stages, we become better settled in the bedrock of how we feel, and we yearn for relief of that pain. The yearning for peace navigates us to other stages in our own time. It's what takes us from weeping in the night to joy in the morning. It's what allows us to put words together to pray again, to hope again, to love again, to believe again.

The Bible shows us numerous instances of people who experienced grief. In their own way, they show that the process of overcoming grief is never singular but includes plural stages for healing. These stages are not a rigid roadmap but a framework that helps us understand the emotional chaos that comes with loss. Grief is deeply personal, and no two journeys are the same. Some may linger in one stage, skip other stages, or cycle back and forth between stages. Yet what unites us is that grief, in all its forms, demands to be felt.

Denial: Shielding Ourselves from the Pain

Denial is one of the first stages in coming to terms with loss. Kübler-Ross[5] noted that "Patients would often reject the reality of the new information after the initial shock of receiving a terminal diagnosis." It is the mind's strategy to cushion the blow, to let us sit with whatever is too overwhelming to grasp. In this stage, the world may seem like it's passing you by, as though the loss hasn't actually occurred. It's the mind's effort to soften the blow, to provide time to absorb what feels too overwhelming to accept all at once. When the doctor confirmed I would need surgery, I still believed that they would go in and find nothing, that this was all a misunderstanding or a misdiagnosis. This was a reaction designed to protect, one that I had built for decades to shield me from pain. I just wouldn't let the full weight of reality in this situation hit me at that time.

---

5 Kübler-Ross, E., & D. Kessler. (2005). *On Grief and Grieving: Finding the Meaning of Grief through the Five Stages of Loss.* Scribner.

Denial works like a circuit breaker in our emotional system. Jennifer Fisher[6] mentions that denial is not a matter of not understanding, but rather, a defense mechanism that is set up to protect oneself. The mind has built-in defenses when it's being swamped with information that is uncomfortable. It is not a coping mechanism that enables us to sustain a degree of function while slowly adding the truth of death to our awareness. The brain, in its infinite wisdom, knows that we would not be able to bear all of our loss at once without becoming psychologically obliterated.

For those mourning an identity, the end of a profession, a relationship, or a dream, denial frequently shows an inability to accept the change will last forever. A recently divorced person might still wear their wedding ring, a retiree might keep his office space, or someone diagnosed with a chronic illness might make plans as though the diagnosis was speculative instead of permanent. In my own experience of mourning the death of my former self, I navigated through all the versions I felt would pop up if you Googled me. The pastor with all the easy answers. The guy with the big smile holding my parents in photos. The anchor that kept it all together and never spent time falling apart. Denial looked like reimmersing myself in my commitment and my agenda like nothing had happened. Denial had me wiping my tears quickly in public because I didn't want the consoling or the coddling. Denial demanded that I close my eyes and wake up to a new day.

Pastorally, I've learned to see denial more as something to be acknowledged rather than healed. When I'm sitting with families in the hours after a loved one has died, I don't correct them if they start speaking in the present tense about the deceased. A woman grieving for a husband who has died could keep setting the table for two, unable to bear the emptiness in her schedule. A parent mourning a child may not touch anything in his room for months, convinced that it must all be some terrible error. I am not in a hurry to take the photographs down or to collect the personal items that are "getting in the way of acceptance." Instead, I believe—or prefer to believe—that these denials are sacred pauses, places visited to find solace before venturing for-

---

6 Fisher, J. (n.d.). *5 Stages of Grief: Coping with the Loss of a Loved One.* Harvard Health Publishing. https://www.health.harvard.edu/mind-and-mood/5-stages-of-grief-coping-with-the-loss-of-a-loved-one

ward again, pursued by our shadows. The psalmist says in Psalm 121:3, "He will not suffer thy foot to be moved: he that keepeth thee will not slumber," and I have come to believe that denial is one way God watches over us, not allowing us to slip into the abyss of despair before our soul has the necessary spiritual muscle to carry the weightiness of our sorrow.

Although denial has a protective feature, it cannot and should not be one's place of permanent existence. There does come a time when further denial is a larger issue, when it stands in the way of the work of grief we must do, and our ability to make new attachments and create new meanings in our different world. The trick is learning to recognize the difference between healthy, temporary denial that soothes our emotional survival and unhealthy, enduring denial that condemns us to continue living in limbo.

Denial serves a purpose. It's where we're given space to breathe when the full weight of reality becomes unbearable. Denial is not an enemy of healing. It's the first friend on the road to wholeness. In understanding its higher purpose, recognizing its manifestations, and respecting its protective role, we can cooperate with denial rather than fight it, leaving it to do its merciful work as we remain open to the slow, gentle rise of acceptance, which comes not by brash coercion but by grace.

Anger: A Fierce Expression of Pain

As denial wanes, the energy of denial turns into anger. This is a raw, hot stage, full of questions that have no answers: Why did this happen? Who is to blame? How can the world do this to me? Anger provides a way to funnel the overwhelming pain we feel about what has happened, even if the rage seems misplaced or irrational. But for a lot of people who are grieving, anger seems like the most dangerous and unwelcome guest in an already oppressive mourning ritual. We fear its power, its mystery, and, most of all, its contradiction to our understanding of faith, love, and healing.

In everyday life, anger may look like testiness with loved ones, frustration at little inconveniences, or anger at the person who is gone. A widower could feel rage toward his late spouse for abandoning him, even though his rational mind says it wasn't their doing. While anger may be isolating, it's also an indication that we're finally beginning to face the reality of our lost love.

Anger in mourning is not frustration or disappointment. Rather, it's a primal, existential rage not at what was done but at the very order of things. It's as if the entire mental psyche is having an allergic reaction to all its basic assumptions about life, safety, and meaning suddenly being undermined. When we lose someone we love, when our identity is taken from us, when our carefully rendered universe is destroyed, anger is the fuel of our souls to rise up. It's almost like the emotional equivalent of a body rejecting a foreign object, struggling with its presence, and refusing to accept it.

I found that after my surgery, the frustration washed over me in waves. I would attempt to write notes to communicate what I was feeling, but none of them quite captured the nuance of what I was trying to say. Texts were average, generic, and impersonal. Failing to capture the warmth, tone, the "*je ne sais quoi*" of my voice. The annoyance and frustration of not being able to do the little things turned into anger. Sometimes I felt bad about being angry, but I could not show it. I didn't want to seem ungrateful that I still had life, but the quality felt fleeting.

There is one distinct moment I recall from my recovery. A friend popped by to lend support and boost my spirits. They talked away, telling stories, asking questions. I smiled, I nodded, and gestured where I could. But through it all, I was screaming for them to just stop. I wanted so badly for someone to see that I wasn't OK, but nobody heard my scream for help. As bad as I wanted to laugh with a person, introduce them to what I was thinking, or even let them know how much their act of kindness or service meant to me, I couldn't. Instead, I felt stuck and afraid that my voice, the thing that made me who I was, was trapped just out of reach.

Prayer, my lifeline in times of difficulty, had moments of feeling futile. I prayed, silently, but I missed hearing the sound of my voice calling out to God. I just wanted the release of talking, hearing my own heart pour itself out to him. In this palace of rage, the questions began to bubble out, misdirected, yet still full of feeling. Is there no other way for me to be well than to lose my voice? Why didn't the medication save my parents? Why did He force me to return to the frightening silence I had only known when my parents and brothers died? This anger felt human, it felt justified, yet especially conflicting as a pastor. How could I be angry at the God I have been placed on Earth to serve? How could I find the means to be thankful for a situation that caused me so much pain? I was angry, I was raw, and I was hurt.

Elisabeth Kübler-Ross mentioned, "Anger is a necessary stage of the healing process. Be willing to feel your anger, even though it may seem endless. The more you truly feel it, the more it will begin to dissipate and the more you will heal."

Anger in grief seldom falls where it belongs. It lies within the very fact that death is unfair, that it's avoidable, that life is as tenuous as it is beautiful, and that there is no master hand on the wheel. Rather, it hunts down far more concrete prey, and in doing so ends up cutting a swathe of relational devastation that re-compounds our original loss with a heap of secondary losses.

I would become angry at doctors who hadn't been able to save my loved one, family members who weren't grieving the way I was, friends who carried on while I was lost in grief. In coming to understand the layers and perils of grief, I found that anger is often directed inward, mutated into a brutal self-criticism that is equally harmful to what we say or do as a result of our anger. But what lingers over us and fuels that under us is guilt. All the things for which we feel responsible, the questions that ring in our minds, become the foundation of this anger. Wondering why we weren't there at the time of their death, didn't say the right words, weren't an adequate son, daughter, spouse, or friend—these sort of questions ate at me, and instead of addressing them, they fueled my anger. This self-directed fury simmered and became rage. The inability to control my own mortality, the inability to control the uncontrollable, left me with a void that I had no other way to address than to be angry.

But in the silence, I remembered Romans 8:26, "The Spirit itself maketh intercession for us with groanings which cannot be uttered. We do not know what we ought to pray for, but the Spirit himself intercedes for us through wordless groans." It wasn't wrong for me to be angry. The psalms are full of this candid fury. David asking in Psalm 13:1, "How long wilt thou forget me, O Lord? forever? how long wilt thou hide thy face from me?" and in Psalm 10:1, "Why standest thou afar off, O Lord? why hidest thou thyself in times of trouble?"

We as humans, Christians, even in our grief, can become sacredly angry. It's the soul's way of saying that something has happened—that love exists, that loss is real. Sometimes, no anger means no connection. Some people skip the anger step initially, but then they fluctuate in and out of this stage throughout their process. Our anger is proof that we love, proof that what has happened to us matters, that it is deserving of deep feeling.

The trick is to learn to respect our anger without being ruined by it, to express it without destroying ourselves or someone else. This is what I refer to as "loving, divine venting." It's a place that, when accessed, allows our anger to be acknowledged, expressed, and soothed. For some, this may involve yelling into pillows, writing angry letters that you never send, pushing hard during workouts, or going axe throwing. For others, it might be honest prayer, kneeled crying and moaning, or working with a therapist who sees the spiritual dimensions of grief. These are all ways that one may navigate the venting to relieve anger.

The psalms allow us to take the rawness of our emotions—may it be anger or anguish or gratitude—to reconcile with God and his will, to fight with the divine in ways that seem to come closer to Jacob's wrestling with the angels. The moment I gave myself permission to pray my anger, to tell God what I really thought of all I'd been through, to ask why, even though I knew full well I'd never get a direct answer, I still found that prayer was big enough to handle my fury. It was enough to keep me in touch with my feelings without expressing them in futility or misdirection.

The anger we vent in grief becomes restorative. Not restorative of the things that are taken from us, but restorative of our ability to love, our ability to hope, our ability to live fully in the world once more. Anger, when rightly dealt with, burns away that flotsam of denial and makes room for the deeper work of mourning. It is the fire that scorches the Earth to allow for new growth, the storm that clears the air for brighter skies. In learning to value our anger without falling under its spell, we learn that anger—our own and that of others—can also be a doorway into healing, a bridge between the world of raw pain and the world of new possibility.

Bargaining: Searching for Control

Bargaining is the phase in which we tussle with the "what-ifs" and "if-onlys." It speaks to our yearning to regain some semblance of control in a world where we feel utterly powerless. At this point, deals are often made. We make promises to ourselves, God, or one another, things that are likely to be temporary, but occasional, salving comforts. Believe me, I've been there, and bargaining is what sneaks in once we start to feel we have any kind of power to control the outcome of a situation. This is where we first start to digest where we are, standing at the crossroads of what was and what must now be, throwing down bad with what we carry around with us like we are owed salvation or something.

The bargaining that emerges in response to a loss can have a very diverse appearance, but the basic pattern of the process is often relatively stereotypical. The essence of bargaining is a desire to make a deal and to regain control over things outside of our control. In some attempts this is to find a way, however narrow, to regain what we are losing. Those are the deals we make, and they speak volumes about our desperation and our love.

For instance, someone whose loved one is dying might pray, "If you let them live, I'll turn my life around for good." Or the person who is angry about a missed opportunity may think, *If only I would have said this or done that, things would be different.* Bargaining is the point at which we really know what we want, but we also begin to move just the tiniest bit along the path of accepting that we can't get what we want.

And the worst part of bargaining is that it's the slow realization that the math of loss doesn't add up quite the way we desperately wish it did. Good behavior isn't going to bring the dead back. And, unfortunately, no amount of self-development work can fix a marriage or relationship that the other partner isn't working on too. The economy of grief deals in another currency than the markets that matter to us, and the currency we offer is always, inevitably, counterfeit.

The weight of those failures can be crushing. We add shame to the original wound, our own guilt over the fact that we cannot pay for the cure. The bargaining is to cycle us into what amounts to a second loss—the loss of that faith that we have in our own ability to fix things. The reality is we are not in control, losing control, and never were in control. Over time, because our attempts to change the unchangeable are not working, we slowly begin to make peace with reality as it is—not as we would like it to be but as it is. We may not be fully at the place of acceptance, but we're sitting with the fact that we have to learn to live on with this new reality. It never goes away. It becomes the new part of us we have to accept.

What is so painful about bargaining is the slow realization that the math of loss doesn't add up. It does not operate the way we so desperately need it to. Nothing is going to bring the dead back, no matter how good you are, so why bother? Nothing can return your previous spouse to you. And transforming yourself into a better you can't fix what has already ended. There is no sacrifice you can make that will reverse a diagnosis and return you to the person you were. The economy of grief does not function according to the laws that govern the markets that we know, and we do not have enough, ever, and are therefore bound to always lack enough to face the bill of life and loss we must pay.

The loss from these failed negotiations can be devastating. In addition to the primary deficit, we have the deficit of ourselves, the fact that we can do nothing to regain what has been lost. And this second loss, the loss of our belief that we can make things better, can be as unsettling as the main loss. It reminds us on an existential level of our weakness, our death, and the radical uncertainty that rules human life.

But it is in the crushing weight that bargaining actually starts to do its most valuable work. As we struggle to change the rollback of the unchangeable, we start the painful, heartbreaking but redemptive process of reconciling ourselves to reality as it is rather than as we would give almost anything for it to be. But in short, this is not acceptance. We're not ready to say we accept our loss. But here we begin the delicate task of figuring out how to live with it.

This process of restitution is frequently a process of switching our deals from the undoable to the doable. Instead of pleading for resurrection, we start to plead for peace. Now, instead of bargaining for the return of our old lives, we begin to beg for the strength to build new ones. Instead of expecting the world to be what we want, we slowly turn and begin to see what kind of life is possible once we fully accept what it is. At the deepest level, bargaining serves to bring us eventually to surrender. Not the surrender of defeat but the happy surrender to the highest place for our concern, our Father who art in Heaven. That surrender is ironic, in that it usually comes from the very act of attempting to stay in control. And it is only when we have run out of bargaining that we come to the peace that passes understanding.

The weight of bargaining in grief is, finally, the weight of our humanity. It's the way we love so much the thing or person we've lost that we want to defy the force that has taken it, so we creatively try to wrest agency in impossible circumstances. It's a sensational education that some things will never change, some losses will never be undone, and some questions will never be negotiated into awareness. But it is also the weight of finding out that we can live through the breaking of our bargains, that there is a sort of peace that exists without our being able to dictate terms and that love.

Depression: Sitting with the Reality

Depression frequently emerges when the loss is fully absorbed. The denial has given way, as it always does, to the anger and bargaining. To the question of "if only," to the sense of futility and waste. But, eventually, to the awful truth. This stage is not the same thing as clinical depression, although the emotions can feel equally burdensome.

As I recovered from my surgery, my isolation became depression. It stung the most because I had felt separated from what made me more colorful and vivid, my voice. And chats with friends and family, once a comforting distraction, became a one-way street. Folks would chat me up, but without my voice in the mix, something was markedly off. I depended on my voice in my work in an array of ways, whether for pitching ideas, for working with colleagues, or for being heard. I felt sidelined, irrelevant and impotent. This feeling festered day by day, a simmering resentment that my body had betrayed me and that my circumstances had consigned me to muteness.

Psalm 6:6 became my lament: "I am weary with my groaning; all the night make I my bed to swim; I water my couch with my tears." Some nights the silence was so thick I cried myself to sleep out of sheer exhaustion. My physical recovery was secondary to the emotional damage, because when I was healing my vocal cords, I wasn't just losing the gift of speech. I was mourning a piece of myself. It was a hard pill to swallow, a pain that sank deep within me. I failed to have the answers for alleviating my pain, and emotional isolation became my safe space.

At this stage, something as simple as a day of life can seem meaningless. One person's depressive grieving may show up in being unable to force themselves out of bed, and another might want to get out of bed. Some will let their responsibilities slip, while others will pull away from friends and family. For instance, there was a time I thought about not attending family functions or gatherings that I knew my mother would have loved to attend. I considered those visits to be too painful without the usual presence of the bedrock of my family.

After my surgery, I often sat in dark rooms, looking for a space that was as silent as I was. I was trying to find an atmosphere that fit the bleakness and fear that continued to sneak into my mind from time to time. In those moments, I found that depression is not something to feel ashamed about, nor is it a bad word that is not to be mentioned. It's not a weakness as many of us are told, nor is it an illness that only medication can treat. I had to unlearn these myths myself, as I was taught varying things about depression. These teachings both formally and culturally made me opposed to the thought that this was even possible. In unlearning former understandings of it, I found the most valuable step was to redefine this step for my healing.

I thought of it instead as the "Valley Stage." I say this because it is in this space that you encounter what may feel like rock bottom, the lowest of low. The nature of grief-based depression is different from other forms because this is where the spiritual and physical often meet up with one another. This paces the slowing-down, which can feel unproductive in a world that worships efficiency and going forward. During times when I didn't have any words, well-meaning friends would tell me what I should "do instead" or the ways in which I should "keep it positive." But what I was learning, in my stretched silent state, was that some healing cannot occur when we are busy. Some transformations require us to stop, to stop moving, to stop producing, to stop being useful in all the ways that we have defined ourselves.

The Bible is full of images of valleys of darkness, trial, and renewal. For instance, in Psalm 23:4, "Yea, though I walk through the valley of the shadow of death, I will fear no evil: for thou art with me; thy rod and thy staff they comfort me." It does not detail an opportunity to go around it, over it, or above it, but through it. This is the language that tells us that the valley isn't a detour from our spiritual journey but a part of it. The depression phase of grief is our strange, shadowy valley of the shadow of death, where we encounter the darkest part of what it means to be without, to deal with loss, and to internalize pain.

In my silence I learned what the men and women of the Bible already knew, that God frequently says his best through people who are too broken to speak a word. God was not in the earthquake or fire, the Prophet Elijah learned, but in the "still, small voice" that followed the storm. (1 Kings 19:12)

My imposed stillness turned into an honesty chamber, a space in which I no longer had the means of performing my faith through preaching and teaching but could only face it in the raw silence of loss. The depression of loss is so often this kind of forced aching, this unwilling breaking down that allows grace to flow into us in ways our supposedly former strength and independence have rendered impossible.

As the mood descends, something small starts to change. The more acute pain of loss doesn't go away. It gradually shifts in quality. It's not a dramatic transition, more like the subtle moment when the days just start to feel a bit longer as winter surrenders to spring. But we can gradually begin to envision a future that doesn't hinge on recovering what we've lost.

For me, this change started when I could no longer understand my silence as simply lack of a voice, but my own unique method of communicating. I learned to care in presence, offer comfort with absence of pomp, engage in worship by listening rather than leading. They were not recompenses for what I had unwillingly lost. They were new competencies, which could only be developed after the patterns of the familiar order of things had been disrupted.

From the depression stage we learn that healing is not about going back to being who we were before the loss. It is about finding out who we can be, after loss has changed us. This means a rethinking of priorities and aspirations. Instead of focusing on restoration, we start working ourselves toward transformation. Rather than attempting to fill the void that we feel with our missing loved one, we learn to live in a great space around it.

Acceptance: The Alignment of Two Opposing Truths

The great myth about acceptance is that a person "gets over" the loss or they should "get over" the loss. Acceptance is not about "getting over" a loss, but about learning how to live with it. Both professionally and personally, when I have seen acceptance, I often see attempts at this early. These early attempts are usually an effort made by people to convince themselves and those around them that they are moving on, free from pain, and without the need to be "fixed." But the truth is, rushing to accept the loss does not fill the void any faster. This stage is very humbling because it is at this stage that we start to recognize that the hurt may never completely go away, but that it's still possible for life to have purpose and happiness. Acceptance is not grieving. Acceptance is hope.

Our society has a broken thought system about acceptance in grief. The story that to heal is to forget and to be whole is to be released from pain has set a rocky foundation for poor progress. This lie projects that those who grieve correctly "get over" their losses. Society has tricked us into thinking that acceptance is a state where the deceased no longer permeates our thoughts and actions. A state where the part of us that we lost no longer holds any significance. This belief is not only untrue, but it's cruel and unfair to the individual as they navigate this unfamiliar territory. It's also destructive, as it builds the parameters that have become standard for how someone "should" grieve. Additionally, it casts a shadow on those who have difficulty accepting, as if they are "bad grievers." Real acceptance during grief is not letting go but walking forward holding our love and our loss. It is the acknowledgment that we can make a life that is both good and meaningful, a life that does not try to rise above our pain but grows with our pain as part of who we are now.

As I, finally, after days of voicelessness, started to find words again, one of the things I recall most are well-meant congregants and friends, and how "glad" they were that I could "get back to normal." But I'd learned in those months that normal had disappeared for good. As the days drew out, I started viewing the silence in a new light. Instead of something inserted to harm, I realized it had allowed me the opportunity to do something I had needed to for a very long time. It required me to slow down, to hear in a way I never had, and to truly feel a connection with those around me. The little things caught my eye in conversation that never had before. The glow in someone's eyes while talking, the way they paused when speaking, the emotions hidden behind their eyes. It also gave me room for contemplation in the stillness. It was only then that I noticed how much I had taken my voice for granted, how cavalierly I used it, how quickly, without much thought.

Acceptance allows us the opportunity to hold two opposing truths at the same time: our heartbreaking truth and the more hopeful one. The silence taught me to be intentional, to not take any word or bond for granted. The voice that came back was not the same one I knew before. It was softer, more circumspect with words, more respectful of the gravity of silence. I never quite got over the fact that I had lost my old voice, but I learned to live with a new voice, to take the change in meaning rather than mourning the difference.

This distinction is important for the acceptance stage, as it is here one can hold onto the lived and the living and choose to live on in a new future. For instance, consider family members who start scholarships or awareness campaigns in honor of a lost loved one. That isn't them getting over the death, nor is that them moving on. It's the acceptance of the matter and choosing to have their loved one's legacy live on. They have accepted the adjustment they had to make to love their child in another way, through action, through giving, and through making that loved one's presence known in the lives of others. Acceptance is not the end of the relationship with what we have lost. It is the beginning of a new relationship, a bond with absence.

I remember being asked what kept a smile on my face through the darkest of days. I say it's the blessed assurance that I believe. It's the knowledge, paired with the peace and certainty that not only will we make it through our loss, but we will find a way to thrive as a result of the supernatural transformation God has instigated within us. This kind of assurance is not based on denial or on positive thoughts but the reality of having walked through the valley and finding that the hills from whence cometh our help is still there. And that we are stronger than we knew. Love is more enduring than death, and meaning can be found in the most devastating of circumstances.

This assurance grows gradually, through small acts of bravery and tiny, incidental moments of recognition. It could be when we laugh for the first time since our loss and recognize that joy can come again. It may come when we sit with someone else through their grief and realize that our own heartache has transformed into wisdom. It may arise when we go someplace where there was once only sadness and discover that there is now room for both tears and laughter. Each year near the anniversary of my mother's death I feel more tender, more aware of her being missing, but I also take the moment to laugh at the things she would have laughed at and find joy in preparing her favorite meal. The acceptance I've forged doesn't shield me from these waves of fresh mourning, but it assures me that I can surf them without sinking. I realize now that missing her at these times doesn't mean I haven't accepted her death. It means I haven't stopped loving her, and I still carry her on my journey.

In the end, acceptance through grief is a steady discipline of saying yes, not to our losses but to life among our losses. It's the daily insistence in the face of evidence that our lives still matter, that love is still worth pursuing, that meaning can still be found, even in the punches that we never would have chosen. This *yes* is not a single act of acceptance but a discipline we have to practice repeatedly, sometimes by the hour, as we figure out how to live in a world forever changed by absence. Acceptance is the guarantee that we will not only survive our losses but also come to find that we are capable of leading substantive, even joyful, lives in the very act of carrying our grief along with us.

CHAPTER 3

THE IMPORTANCE OF GRIEF

"Why is grief important?" That question lies at the very center of human life and divine design. In this society that often sees grief as an inconvenience to be conquered in quick sprints, we have to recognize that sorrow is an important and essential task for our spiritual, emotional, and relational experiences. Grief is an inevitable part of the human experience, yet a reflection of the loving and connecting nature that holds us together. Although it's often viewed as something we are meant to withstand or flee, grief is important in contributing to who we are. It shares lessons we might never learn otherwise about resilience, empathy, and the depth of our own hearts.

While painful, grief is a necessary part of living, a guide to life, a friend in life. As we go through stages of grieving and struggle, we should bear in mind the purpose of our grief.

Even Jesus showed what an important thing grief is. When Lazarus died, Jesus went to the village of Bethany where he was buried. When Jesus saw Martha and the other villagers weeping, He wept. Their grief over Lazarus's passing touched him. The astonishing thing is, Jesus knew he was going to rescue Lazarus from the dead, but he willingly indulged in the sorrowfulness of the incident. Those two words "Jesus wept" grant us permission to weep in our sorrow, because they show how Jesus modeled that crying in times of grief is normal. Let's not give in to the belief that it's more spiritual to hold in your tears than to release them as an expression of surrender.

When pain serves society's best interest and seeking comfort is its highest ambition, the act of choosing to assign grief significance is countercultural and prophetic. Some things are too precious to avoid, some lessons too important to omit, and some changes too vital to cut out. Though mourning the loss of those closest to me has been the worst pain I have ever suffered by far, I have learned along the way, and I remain hopeful that life will continue to allow people to experience grief.

I kept my voice alive for more than just someone else's body. It was something I was very much focused on as a ministry tool, a means by which I found connections, ways to show care for and comfort others. Without it, I lost a very important part of how I navigated the world. But once I permitted myself to grieve, to experience the gravity of what I lost, everything shifted. I cried on and on and on over sermons I couldn't preach, people with whom I could not otherwise have discussions. Perhaps most difficult of all, I couldn't speak normally to pray to God. It left me feeling as though I was not fulfilling my purpose as his vessel. I mourned everything of my identity that had been built around it and more, but it was not just in my cries for my own voice. It was also loss.

The heartbreak of this was aching but also enlightening. It taught me all sorts of things I never would have known while I tried to work through my deficits. I found that my desire to always have the right words could be paralyzing, when I was simply there to sit with people's distress. Without the words of the past, I learned a ministry of silence, of holding space without trying to fill it. I experienced how much a part of my pastoral identity had been built on performance, rather than presence. The grief stripped away the impressiveness or persuasiveness of my ability to articulate and showed me a starker call to love—to love a man, woman, or child as they are.

I concluded that vulnerability could be a more powerful form of ministry than competence. People related to my struggle in ways they had never connected with my strength. But most of all, I've learned that grief does not go ignored. The pain I had tried to escape by living a busy, "positive" life grew more painful, until I gave it the careful handling it required. But when I took the time to honor my grief, when I felt like it mattered and wasn't just an inconvenience, it was less a hindrance than a teacher.

On the tenth day, when I began speaking again, the sound of my voice was far from my own. It was cracked and wavered, but it was mine. I started crying, and I whispered a small *thank you* to God, heavy with gratitude for something I previously thought I could never lose. That experience changed me. It allowed me to empathize more deeply with people who live alone in silence for physical, emotional, and sometimes social reasons. It was a powerful reminder of the power of presence, that even just showing up for someone, say, in silence, can speak volumes.

I was living the experience of Isaiah 40:31: "But they that wait upon the Lord shall renew their strength; they shall mount up with wings as eagles; they shall run, and not be weary; and they shall walk, and not faint." Even if I experienced fatigue, God gave me a new strength I had never dreamed of, teaching me in the silence. In those moments, I had to submit to the lesson, his will, and settle into the silence to realize the value and significance of this moment. I had to process emotions that were exhausting.

This was one of the hardest paths to travel, but it was important for the process. There are profound understandings to be realized in this season of deconstruction. Now, with the familiar threads of our identity ripped away by loss, and the comforts of our everyday existence uprooted by a grief-shaking eruption, we cannot find an education like this: we cannot study through books, with a lesson no longer available to us. We must live through our walk down the valley of shadows of grief, yet fear not the experience because thou are with us.

The Lessons Grief Teaches

A lesson is a teaching or learning opportunity. We have limited learning opportunities in our day-to-day within educational spaces that we can then avoid learning in our spaces. The first lesson learned is that grief *demands* that we feel. In a culture where many of us are placed in a comfort zone, the less comfortable a scenario, the less we wish to engage with that discomfort. In the space of grief, it is difficult to learn, as it requires us to stop and face the essence of our feelings. It exposes our pain in an honest but painful manner that we may not otherwise acknowledge. It brings us closer to the essence of our pain. I learned to embrace vulnerability and understand that pain is not something to be afraid of but rather requires awareness and then acceptance.

Secondly, the pain of grief requires empathy. It allows us to learn about others and the things they endure. It makes us consider how we can help them in that moment of our life. It calls us to pour out without assuming we will have anything poured back in. To instead push us to be deliberate about sources of renewal, not in people but in our faith. For me, grief erased the illusion of control and humbled me. It had, and has, become a reminder of how precious everything in life truly is. It revealed how empathy should guide everything I did, thought, and felt. The loved ones we share relationships with, the memories we make, and the connections we create are limited by time. Our recognition of this, of the beauty we share in loss, deepens the reality that time is fleeting, so we lack the time to dwell on frustrations, disdains, and disagreement.

In nature, it's where organic matter has decomposed that the richest soil is created. Death comes before life, leaving room for new beginnings through endings. Farmers understand that compost, which compounds the dead and degenerate from what was once present, is the best base for future growth. The same dynamic has its roots in the human heart. Grief provides soil for the composted soul, rich soil in which fresh growth can sprout.

Consider how the fire has responded to a forest, for example. So much of what looks like destruction is revival beneath disguise. There are seeds lying in wait on the forest floor for years, waiting for the fire to crack their shells and allow them to germinate. The ash left behind following the flames ensures that necessary nutrients are obtained, promoting new growth. Some species have no means of reproduction without fire. They have evolved to depend on what looks like their own destruction for survival. There is a time to plant and a time to uproot, suggesting that proper growth cannot occur without cultivation, but equally so, it cannot occur without letting go.

Thirdly, grief is our time of uprooting, a painful but necessary phase for gaining new knowledge, kindness, and life experiences. The person who begins suffering deeply in their grieving is not the same person who will emerge from it. As a forest grows in different and resistant ways, so does the grieving person. As I lost my voice during those seven months of silence, I began to learn the ways what looked like the end of my main instrument for ministry was opening up new paths of connection and service. Much like seeds of seeds, which I buried so much in the subconscious, new gifts began to blossom. My listening deepened, family and friends who surrounded me grew evermore present, and my own ability to draw comfort beyond the spoken word deepened. Grief hollowed out the strengths I had depended on before and opened other strengths that I would not have realized that I had.

Lastly, grief is about articulating what was and about understanding that something is missing and saying, "This mattered." To grieve is to recognize that a person, or a thing, meant something, that they touched the fabric of our lives. And now that they are no longer here, how do we make sense of what's left? We document what we once possessed right within the holy land of mourning.

I also wanted to underscore that there is an opposite to grief, and that is love. To this point, sorrow is so emotional. Grief is the fruit of suffering that you keep at, and take up through, and change your life. It honestly says that what mattered and was intimate—even if not according to our expectations—was about the love we're able to remember. We live in an era of collective love, when the love expressed isn't necessarily based on outward displays of love or gaudy displays of love, but in an inner sense. Grieving feels very distinct, something that's powerful, profoundly revealing, and, at the end of it, sacred.

Our losses are strength, not a sign of weakness or lack of closeness, but of how deeply we have fallen in love. Just as a seismograph uses lines and strokes to detail the severity of an earthquake, grief expresses and documents the waves of love that used to flood our lives. Grief, this was the love in such heavy expression, and now the strength of our grief is the very strength of our love. For both, the ability to mourn indicates one's capacity for love. Both capacities express God inside of us.

When we mourn, we mourn not only what we lost, but also what we can offer in our lives as we go on to honor them and cherish the space they held in our hearts. Honoring the love that once enriched us as something beyond ourselves as individuals. To show the depth of our love, grief reveals the depth of our humanity, the magnificence of our connections, and the worth of every heart that has loved another for so long that on losing them, it feels like every aspect of our inner self has died. Grieving doesn't mean forgetting or giving up things. It is honoring the space that what we loved used to fill. It's remembrance, with reverence, with tears sometimes, with silence. The depth of our sorrow is proportional to the intensity of our contact with the person or thing we love. Grief is love's price, and the fullest acceptance of it teaches us where our love lies. Embracing that love, we can also realize our love. It is a reminder that despite the loss of a beloved life, there is still love that transcends and endures in life beyond death.

Processing Emotions Through Grief

I have learned that grief is more than just sadness. It encompasses a complex mix of emotions, including anger, guilt, confusion, and sudden moments of happiness. Each of these feelings contributes to the overall experience of grief. The pain associated with each emotion has its place in the grieving process. All must be felt and acknowledged. Processing emotions in response to loss holds significant value. It is not optional work that we can defer indefinitely, nor is it self-indulgent wallowing without purpose. Instead, it is essential labor that, when approached courageously and intentionally, transforms our understanding of loss and enhances our capacity for being human.

The time we spend grieving enables our emotions to breathe. To process emotions through grief is to tear down the walls we've built from other people's expectations and our own fears of being "too much." It's messy and it's raw, and it refuses to perform. Because grief isn't a performance. It's the emotional price we pay for having loved, and it demands to be honored on its own terms, not society's. It allows us to incorporate the reality of our evolution into our sense of self and opens the door for new forms of love and meaning to emerge. We cry because the pain is too much to contain.

We rage because the loss feels unfair. We laugh at a recollection because it offers a brief respite from tragedy. These expressions pave the way for healing by releasing the energy of our pain, moment by moment.

Emotions are not neutral. They never truly cease but transform when we engage with them. Sadness may evolve into tenderness. Anger can turn into a passion for justice. Fear might develop into wisdom about vulnerability. The nature of our feelings changes, becoming less reactive and more responsive, less overwhelming and more informative, hence the importance of the process.

I used to think that crying about my parents, my brothers, and other loved ones was the only emotional processing I needed to navigate losing them. However, over time, I realized that a good cry was important in expressing what I was experiencing instead of simply labeling it as "grief." I was sad, hurt, angry, desperate, and much more. The emotions tied to grief are not the same as feelings experienced solely in grief. We *experience* emotions constantly, often in fleeting ways as reactions to our current circumstances. But *processing* emotions is deeper. It requires a willingness to sit with our feelings long enough to understand what they are communicating to us. It involves tracing their roots and allowing their transformative power to wash over us.

Some tools I found useful while processing:

> ***Journaling*** – Write freely about feelings, memories, and thoughts without censoring. Also, allow yourself to see the development of your emotions. Paper and pen allow you an unfiltered and unjudged space to be honest about your aches, while invoking the freedom to process.
>
> ***Naming the Feeling*** – Name and acknowledge emotions as they arise ("I'm feeling angry right now" or "I'm feeling happy"). Putting words to how you feel helps you to process and not fall into blanket terms like "I'm okay." Be honest about where your grieving journey is taking you. I had grown to a place where I could not mask every feeling or emotion as being "okay." The word okay became a lie, especially on the days and moments when I was struggling to keep it all together.

> ***Letter writing*** – I wrote letters to my loved ones, and in some instances to the loss itself. Write letters to your future self or your past self, confirming that there will be hope and happiness again, or that you will see your loved one again. Letter writing allows you to speak to those parts of us that we feel we have to suppress. Furthermore, it allowed me to process without fear of judgment that I was not being fair, or that I didn't have it all together. It is a raw and uncut opportunity to express where you are and where you hope to be. Your letter may be to God, a written expression of your prayer when the words may be too painful to say, yet still worth making known to the Lord.

Perhaps the most important lesson processing grief teaches is compassion—not the theoretical understanding of suffering but the visceral knowledge that comes only through personal experience. Grief initiates us into what Henri Nouwen called "the fellowship of suffering,"[7] connecting us to the vast community of human beings who have faced loss and found ways to carry it meaningfully.

This ability to feel compassion is not discovered through study or observing. It necessitates walking straight through our own valley of shadows. As medical students must undergo clinical rotations to earn their license to serve, so must we, as grieving patients, undergo grief rotations to become adequately qualified healers to help those hurting in a broken world. The Apostle Paul recognized this when he wrote in 2 Corinthians 1:4, "Who comforteth us in all our tribulation, that we may be able to comfort them which are in any trouble, by the comfort wherewith we ourselves are comforted of God."

This new vision is one of grief's most profound gifts. It develops what I call "wounded vision"—the ability to recognize the subtle signs of suffering in others. For instance, the slight hesitation before answering "How are you?" or the forced brightness of a smile that doesn't reach the eyes, the way someone holds their body when they're carrying invisible weight. Those

---

7 Nouwen, Henri J. M. *The Wounded Healer: Ministry in Contemporary Society.* Garden City, NY: Doubleday, 1972.

who have grieved deeply develop an almost supernatural sensitivity to these signals because they have learned to read them in themselves.

The parent who has lost a child develops a radar for other grieving parents that cannot be replicated through training. The person who has survived divorce can offer hope to others facing marital breakdown in ways that married counselors, however skilled, simply cannot. The individual who has grieved the loss of career, health, or identity becomes a guide for others navigating similar transitions.

This compassion extends beyond human relationships to include all of creation. Grief often awakens us to the interconnectedness of all life, the way that loss in one part of the system affects the whole. We begin to see our personal losses as part of the larger pattern of suffering and renewal that characterizes existence itself. This expanded awareness often leads to environmental consciousness, social justice advocacy, and other forms of care for the wounded world.

The Danger of Suppressing Grief

When one suppresses grief, it does not vanish. It simply hides under layers of other stuff. People who repress their feelings of grief say they feel trapped, never free to move on or experience happiness. This emotional deadness leaves you feeling secluded, depressed, or extremely disconnected. The challenge of processing our feelings through grief is not about saying we're over it, and we are done, but it's about how we come to live with it, how we carry it forward, all without losing ourselves in it.

The source of suppression is often fear. The fear of being overwhelmed, the fear of succumbing to the pain, the fear of being unable to control one's own life or feeling weak, or the fear of being labeled weak because we fall apart. But when grief is suppressed, it will always take on other forms in the way it presents itself. It may show itself in the form of anger, restlessness, or constant anxiety. It makes relationships strained because the unprocessed pain distances us from the people who love us.

In our culture's quest for productivity and perfection, grief is considered an unwanted disruption. As we look around, we have constructed a society that is comfortable with almost every conceivable emotion but grief, every instinctive reaction except the natural human reaction to loss. That pressure to "bounce back," to "stay strong," and "move on," morphs our experience of grief into a dirty secret, nothing but an expression of weakness, rather than a reflection of love. But when we repress our grief and when we deny its urgency, when we refuse to affirm its onset, refuse to acknowledge its essential and uncomfortable presence, or ignore its uncomfortable truths, we do nothing more than create emotional damage to our soul.

As a river that has been dammed, grief doesn't go away when we stop its regular flow. It taps into different channels, causing unforeseen catastrophes in parts of our lives that appear completely disconnected from the original loss. Depression is the most widely used disguise for unexpressed grief. While the natural sadness of healthy grieving comes in waves and fades over time, the depression that is caused by the suppressed grief is always chronic and widespread. It doesn't have the recognizable line to loss typical of normal grief, and it is harder to understand or even treat. The individual may experience profound sadness, emptiness, hopelessness, and is unable to explain why. That is because the true loss has been buried so deeply, and the conscious mind has lost track of it.

Anxiety can be another mask for unacknowledged grief.[8] When this becomes our normal practice, if we can't confront the reality of loss, we will continue to struggle with an almost unbearable discomfort. Anxiety rears its head in the overthinking, in the panic of not reaching other loved ones, in the unsettling that is the pain that comes along for the ride. This is the anxiety that accompanies the unprocessed recognition that something terrible has happened and there was a great loss.

It is easy to choose whether we are going to try to wall off grief and cope with its cascading force in the lives of our bodies, minds, relationships, and spirits, or if we are going to learn to recognize and honor loss as a sacred process that should always exist. We can help to maintain that cultural

8 Smith, C. B. (2018). *Anxiety: The Missing Stage of Grief: A Revolutionary Approach to Understanding and Healing the Impact of Loss.* Da Capo Lifelong Books.

conspiracy of denying authentic emotion, or we can help model a different kind of being human—one where all human experience is regarded as holy and necessary. This is not just a personal but a prophetic choice.

In a world where values are, more than ever, being driven by efficiency over depth, productivity over process, positivity over authenticity, grieving well is a cultural act in opposition. It declares love is more important than comfort, truth is more significant than convenience, and becoming truly human is more important than looking good.

The hazards of denying grief are numerous and real, but they are also not inescapable. When we confront our grief, and then opt to process our grief honestly and fully; if we feel (and feel our pain deeply) fully, we are not only reconciling ourselves, but we are also opening possible channels for healing in our families, communities, and culture. We become living testimonies to the truth that we can carry loss, without it crumpling us, experience pain without its obliteration, and grieve in ways that ultimately will lead us not into the depths of despair with pain, but to deeper love, a clearer heart, and a more genuine hope.

I learned that grieving is a kind of sacrifice. In any relationship or dynamic where one has to make sacrifices, the main ingredient is bravery. It requires faith that it is possible to make it through this season. Though it doesn't always have that appearance in the moment, it is true. To partake in the process is to sit with our hurt, to see it directly, and engage in a dance of steps and missteps, sometimes getting them all right and on other days not doing anything at all. We do this because we give ourselves what we think is a shot at healing. We come to realize that our emotions, however intense, will not ruin us. They are also part of us, and they are a testament to our very humanity.

Grief as a Bridge to Connection

Grief is lonely. It would be unfair to say that the grieving experience is full of community warmth and embrace. I often speak about the struggle of grief starting primarily when everyone leaves. And I encourage family and loved ones to not feel that the funeral service or the reception is a time to be the most present. The true value of connection is at the loneliest moments of grief. It is only in our shared experiences of grief that we feel the profound empathy of others. When we tell others about our pain, we allow them to understand and be compassionate. At a time when the world glorifies independence and self-sufficiency, grief does the radical exercise of showing that we are fundamentally intertwined. It removes the mirages of agency and control modern-day life teaches us to expect, revealing that we are relational beings who call on one another not only in times of need but also when survival becomes challenging.

No, grief does not happen only to isolated individuals. It builds communities, builds bonds, and builds bridges that close the chasms of humanity in ways nothing else can. This universality mixed with specificity is the thing that makes grief so powerful a connector. Each loss is a unique form shaped by the specific relationship, the specific circumstances, and the specific human involved. This establishes what psychologists refer to as "common ground."[9] This is a common, shared baseline of experience that enables strangers to become allies, acquaintances to become friends, as well as lone warriors to find their way into a community that transcends the individual. This connection is one of the greatest gifts of grief. It teaches us that we are not alone and that other people have walked this same path and are walking it yet. When we tell our stories, we build bridges of empathy, a sense of belonging, even when we are grieving. This biological need for connection in mourning serves several purposes. It guarantees that the most vulnerable around us, including those weakened by bereavement, are covered in the community and love they need to survive.

It forms the platform for the sharing of both practical and emotional resources. Most of all, it promotes those social ties that improve whole communities' ability to face future challenges. As I went through my own experience of voice loss, I was surprised to find out that my vulnerability was a magnet for others' stories. People who had never spoken of their struggles came to me with stories of loss and limitation. The teenager who had never

9 Clark, H. H., & S. A. Marshall. (1981). "Definite Reference and Mutual Knowledge." In A. K. Joshi, B. Webber, & I. A. Sag (Eds.), *Elements of Discourse Understanding*. Cambridge University Press.

mentioned her learning disability, who struggled to make friends or feel heard and seen by others because of her seclusion and timidness, opened up to me. The businessman who had hidden his bankruptcy for months. The old woman who had been quietly mourning her husband's dementia for years. My visible struggle gave them permission to confront their own, and I was blessed with connections they would not have forged otherwise.

Grief has its own language. It creates a vocabulary of gestures and expressions that convey meaning without words, though we struggle to describe this in language. This language sits beneath the level of conscious communication, providing instant acknowledgment for those who have suffered and those who are suffering. For example, consider how someone who has lost their child can see another bereaved parent across a crowded room, or how those who have been through divorce are able to identify each other's own shade of sorrow.

This sacred language is recognized in scripture throughout its pages. Job's friends, who came to him in distress, "So they sat down with him upon the ground seven days and seven nights, and none spake a word unto him: for they saw that his grief was very great." (Job 2:13) But before they brought up their ultimately unhelpful advice, they conversed beautifully with presence and silence, the language of shared humanity that can be told without words. That's the same principle Paul alludes to when he discusses in Romans 12:15 "Rejoice with them that do rejoice, and weep with them that weep." This is not just emotional mimicry but involvement in a common experience of grief that builds connections that go beyond words. It's about the acknowledgment that, in our pain, we're not alone. We're part of a community of lovers and sorrowers.

In a world where power—especially the ability to suppress all one's suffering—is often mistaken as strength, grief requires a different kind of courage. It requires the courage to face brokenness and the courage to be seen in our brokenness, to confess to our need for help, to recognize that we don't have it all figured out. That enforced vulnerability serves as the key to genuinely connecting in ways that strength and competence never could. Genuine connection isn't about getting it right, says Dr. Brené Brown. In her work on vulnerability, she goes into being able to feel "shame resilience."[10] It's the ability to work through painful emotions without being crushed by them and leaving oneself open to intimacy. Grief offers grueling training in this sort of resilience. It engrains in you the adaptability of being vulnerable and not victimized, broken yet not bitter, needy but never demanding. This vulnerability creates what one might experience as a magnet's pull toward life-giving relationships that welcome our new selves.

There is something inherently attractive about those who can share their story. Because giving people permission to tell their story makes it real. That's why there is so much to be gained from the discomfort and rawness of grief. That perfectly poised person may elicit admiration but not closeness. The person who's visibly working their way through grief, by contrast, is sending a message that you can be human, you can struggle, you can need help, and you can also heal. When we tell our grief stories, we start ripples that reach all our relationships. Every such story of suffering and recovery becomes a resource for others as they attempt one, a map of the terrain that only those who have walked it can tread. Every shared story creates a trail between many bridges: between teller and listener, past experience and present hope, personal suffering and universality, private suffering and public healing.

Not only do these bridges hold information, they also contain the potential for change for all concerned. Grief also broadens our capacity for caring for others. Having survived our own losses, we are better prepared to sit with someone else in their suffering.

I thought I had mastered this until I needed someone to sit with me, to hold my head, to be a shoulder for me to cry on. We know that there are no perfect words, no shortcuts. Instead, there are just simple, powerful acts of showing up. This empathy makes our interactions more real and meaningful. Grief offers one of the deepest truths about human existence: We are not made to confront our deepest concerns alone.

---

10 Brown, B. (2006). "Shame Resilience Theory: A Grounded Theory Study on Women and Shame." *Families in Society*, 87, 43-52.

The ties that take shape in shared sorrow are what I call "sacred circles." They are communities in care that embrace pain and healing, ends and beginnings, death and life. These sacred circles remind us that love is stronger than death, not because it avoids loss but because it produces the bonds that survive loss and multiply via stories shared, comfort offered, bridges built across even the chasm between life and death. And in these communities, we find that our grief does not need to be concealed or overcome but to be shared and transformed through connection with those who understand the weight we bear and what makes that life worth carrying.

I yearned for more than brotherhood, and that is what was formed in my most desolate moments. There was a sacred circle of brothers who called, checked on me, loved, and who sat in the silence. They shared, and I shared, and this action gave me the strength to see that the bridges from this time would last forever.

The bridge builder that is grief not only links us to those who are mourning, it connects us to the human family as a whole, to the greater web of love and grief that runs through time and up to the end of all sorrow. Then we learn as a society to grieve together, how to live together. By sharing our grief together, we live together. We see our lives by sharing our loss, not just with each other, but with the lives of all who live and die. And in the midst of our hurt, in the process of breaking down and becoming bridges, we provide a path to restoration that benefits not just us but everyone who can walk down this path with us. This is grief's ultimate gift: It teaches us that we belong to each other, our sorrows are each other's sorrows, and our healing is the healing of a collective. What we are missing out on is the love that builds grief, the same love that carries us as a people, from the land of loss to the country of renewed life.

The Gift of Grief

Nobody ever sees grief as a gift. When you imagine the aching, the pain, the confusion, the sadness, it's never easy to put grief and gift in the same sentence. Grief isn't a gift we ask for. Still, it is kind of a gift. It constructs us, shows us love, strength, and the interconnectedness of everything. But to call grief a "gift" seems almost to offend others who are living through fresh loss. For example, it is like calling a hurricane refreshing rain or a house fire ambient light. The language has had the effect of minimizing the devastation, of spiritualizing, through which real anguish passes the heart when love intersects loss. But maybe our resistance to seeing grief as a gift stems from our contained conception of what gifts are.

We were conditioned by a consumer society to regard any gift as a pleasant treat, an object to be desired wrapped up in colorful, enticing paper and tied with a perfect bow. We want gifts to make us happy, to free our way into life, to unify our lives and bring peace that isn't complicated.

Take Jesus—he came to bring joy, peace, and favor, but not without pain, suffering, complication, and even sacrifice. Being attached to the shallow understanding of gift-giving smudges the deeper truth that the most transformative gifts are wrapped in suffering, tied with tears, and delivered by circumstances we'd never choose. The present is not a birthday present or a Christmas surprise, but rather, it is the gift of sight to someone born blind and is often terrifying, dizzying, sometimes painful and, finally, revelatory. It is the depth you offer someone who lives only on masks, the authenticity you offer someone who lives in a life of illusion, the empathy you give someone who is insulated by privilege from real life. Each of these gifts comes at a fee for us, for making you go out of your depth into a different person than before, and for developing the capacities you didn't know you needed—for realizing truths that might have been hidden from your view in the past.

Spiritually speaking, grief is amongst life's most reliable awakeners. Through its work with us, it delves deep into the illusions that keep us out of the experience of the ultimate reality. And in a time of relative comfort, we think we, as leaders, are in control. It can be one step nearer to imagining that our plans help to determine the outcome, as if they tell the narratives. Grief tears apart these soothing illusions and exposes the starker truths of spiritual traditions that have long taught that we are not in charge, that we are not independent, that we are held fast by forces beyond our control. This comes about often through what mystics term "the dark night of the soul," during which all our spiritual certainties pale in comparison to what we know as being the world. The prayers that were there with comfort now appear to lift up the empty air above. The Scriptures that once provided answers seem to mock our questions now. Faith, which once felt firm, falls apart in our face like sand. This spiritual disassembly shows not that God abandoned us, but that in our weakest moments it is easy to fall prey to the binds of the flesh and float in the moment.

C. S. Lewis beautifully captured this experience in his *A Grief Observed*, in which he wrote of his wife's death, as he did about God. Saying, "Meanwhile, where is God? This is one of the most disquieting symptoms. When you are happy, so happy that you have no sense of needing Him, so happy that you are tempted to feel His claims upon you as an interruption, if you remember yourself and turn to Him with gratitude and praise, you will be, or so it feels, welcomed with open arms. But go to Him when your need is desperate, when all other help is vain, and what do you find? A door slammed in your face, and a sound of bolting and double bolting on the inside."[11]

But Lewis learned, as many do, that this seeming abandonment was actually an invitation to encounter God, not as a transactional vending machine or divine problem-solver but as the merger of experiences to bring forth the balance of life. The spiritual gift of grief is this deepened understanding of a God big enough to contain our anger, deep enough to contain our despair, and strong enough to endure our doubts.

This deep spiritual awakening through grief often creates what Richard Rohr calls "second-half-of-life spirituality."[12] He describes that in life we encounter two main events. The first half, during which we develop the thing essential for the container, metaphorically what one could consider to be "life" itself. And the second half is spent more focused on its contents. More focused on discovering what that container holds and finding that God enlarges the container with grace. With the faith to shift to the "second-half-of-life spirituality" we grow the courage to abide uncertainty and locate God. It's a spirituality that finds the sacred in the secular, the holy in the shattered, the divine in the heartbroken. Those who receive this

11 Lewis, C. S. (1961). *A Grief Observed*. HarperOne.

12 Rohr, R. (2024). *Falling Upward: A Spirituality for the Two Halves of Life* (Revised and Updated ed.). San Francisco, CA: Jossey-Bass.

gift have frequently said that though they wouldn't pick their losses, they wouldn't exchange the spiritual richness those losses generated for anything.

And in its gift, it leaves us with the opportunity to continually receive. Grief is a teacher. It isn't easy, and it isn't gentle, but its lessons are rich. It beseeches us to feel deeply, to develop in ways we didn't anticipate, and to carry on the love that loss can never rob. It is in the midst of grief that we realize not only the depths of our pain, but also the infinite depths of our hearts. And it is in understanding that we plant the seeds of healing, connection, and hope.

CHAPTER 4

FAITH AS A REFUGE IN GRIEF

When the grief gnawed at my life and left me brokenhearted and wondering where God was, I had more questions than I could count. But as time went on, there were times the words and arms of those around me weren't enough. I yearned for a fulfillment, a way to fill the void that loss had left in me. The loss of my loved ones, my direction, my voice created a void so deep it felt as though nothing could fill it. I wrestled with these feelings, ranging from despair to anger, and I would ask questions I wasn't sure I'd ever get an answer to.

In those early days of loss, prayer became my lifeline. When I couldn't find the words to express the depth of my sorrow, I would simply sit in silence, allowing the tears to flow as I reached out to God. As I navigated my journey, Psalm 34:18 spoke directly to the broken pieces of my heart. As I mentioned before, I visited this verse continually as a reminder. "The Lord is nigh unto them that are of a broken heart; and saveth such as be of a contrite spirit." Through the rain of laments, my faith was a haven, a safe place of peace, strength, and optimism that pulled me above the tide of pain down in the pits of my heart. I recall sitting at church one Sunday, hardly managing to keep it together, when the words of the hymn cradled my heart in its hand and refused to let go.

"Though Satan should buffet, though trials should come
Let this blest assurance control
That Christ has regarded my helpless estate
And hath shed His own blood for my soul."
—Horatio Spafford

There were moments when I doubted this promise. I felt so crushed, so distant from joy, that I wondered if even God could reach me. But as I sat in my pain, pouring out my heart to Him, I began to feel His presence. The words confirmed for me that what I was feeling—the pain, the trials—were not wrong, but that there was regard for me with the only one that could restore my strength. I understood I was not carrying this burden alone. God was there in the stillness, in the tears, in the questions I was reluctant to articulate. Prayer became my lifeline. Not those rehearsed prayers from when I was a kid but raw, honest interactions with God. I confided in Him that I was angry, I was confused, I was afraid that the pain would never end. I didn't conceal my doubts or pretend to have faith that felt more powerful than it was.

I understood scripture in a new way. In my study, I had read this before, but it suddenly spoke right to my wounded heart. "The Lord is close to the brokenhearted and saves those crushed in spirit" was suddenly more than words on a page. It became a promise, my hold on everything else as it got tenuous. Faith was not painless or without doubt, I started to believe. It is to trust in God even when the means to get through is unknown. My church family rallied around me in ways I never could have imagined. Meals appeared at my door. Cards inundated my mailbox with words of encouragement. People sat with me in my grief, not trying to fix it or get me through it, but being present. In their love, support, and encouraging spirit from above, I saw God's hands and his heart in human form.

I learned that faith wasn't just something that happens individually between me and God but was something enacted through people's lives, in how people care for one another in some of life's strongest moments. There were disappointments, of course. Days when the grief seemed as new as it had ever been. Instances where I doubted that I was strong enough not to be crushed. But in each of them, my faith would keep me steady, and my faith would catch me. I started to understand that healing wasn't being able to finish the line to the point the pain left the body entirely. It was dealing with carrying the loss and not stopping, knowing that the Lord was building purpose and contentment out of what He made even through the most painful chapters of my journey. He was moving on.

Grief pushed my faith to being less about knowing all the answers and more about trusting the One who knows. It moved from being strong to being truthful with my weakness. The God I learned to know through my suffering wasn't abstract or indifferent to my pain. He was near, at an even closer distance, walking down the valley with me. This experience of mourning clarified that faith doesn't protect us from pain, but it does sustain us in discomfort. It provides a scaffold at moments everything else has just broken. When things seem hopeless, it brings hope. And it reminds us that even during our worst times, we're never alone.

Wrestling with Questions and Finding Peace

Loss will make you wonder why. Why could they not hold on a while longer? Why did God not heal them? Why would a loving God allow such profound pain? Why take those I loved so deeply? I struggled to reconcile my belief in a good and sovereign God with the reality of my suffering. My wrestling filled me with uncertainty, but also with the guilt that I was questioning the will of God. I feared that he would see me as ungrateful for the time I did have with them. It felt as though all my emotions were together, and they were flowing out of me in waves.

It was during these moments of doubt that I found comfort in the story of David. David, who had navigated instances of loss of physical people and also the loss of titles and respect. In these moments, he cried out to God in anguish, pleading for answers and direction. Pleading that God would find it the opportune time to grant him peace. David faced the death of his infant son with Bathsheba. He faced the loss of the father/son relationship with the betrayal by his own son Absalom, who later died in rebellion against him. He suffered the loss of community as persecution by King Saul forced him into years of exile. The loss of his best friend, Jonathan, and the loss of identity as his name had become tarnished. These experiences of loss led to grief, the pain of injustice, and the anger that we feel in his words in the psalms. Songs that express the full range of human emotion from despair to hope, from anger to worship.

David shows the raw human nature of wrestling with questions and finding peace. David didn't sanitize his pain or pretend to have faith he didn't feel in the moment. Yet, through this honest dialogue with God, David consistently found his way from lament to trust and from questions to peace. His journey shows us that both doubt and faith will present during your cycle of grief. David's example gives us permission to bring our darkest emotions to God, as it is a means of seeking renewal to leave his presence changed. David's story reminded me that faith doesn't mean we have all the answers. Rather, faith is choosing to trust in God's goodness, even when life feels anything but good. Slowly, I began to release my need for answers, finding peace in the knowledge that God's ways are higher than mine. (Isaiah 55:8-9)

David wrestled with questions but ended up on the road to peace. He navigated through:

- **The raw question** – Asked in Psalm 13:1-2 and Psalm 22:1, "How long wilt thou forget me, O Lord? forever? how long wilt thou hide thy face from me?" "My God, my God, why hast thou forsaken me? why art thou so far from helping me, and from the words of my roaring?" and in Psalm 88:14, "Lord, why castest thou off my soul? why hidest thou thy face from me?"
- **The feelings of abandonment** – David described feeling forgotten by God, comparing himself to broken vessels and those already in the grave.
- **The hollowness of despair** – Psalm 88 ends without resolution, showing that some days, grief simply has to be acknowledged without forcing a happy ending.
- **The restoration at the throne of grace** – Didn't hide his anger, confusion, fear, or sense of injustice. He argued with God and demanded to be heard.

- **The memory of God's faithfulness** – Repeatedly recalling what God had done before as in Psalm 77:11: "I will remember the works of the Lord: surely I will remember thy wonders of old."
- **The faith to trust God despite circumstances** – Made deliberate declarations of faith, even when feelings hadn't caught up: "Yet I will rejoice in the Lord, I will joy in the God of my salvation." (Habakkuk 3:18, though written by Habakkuk, reflects David's pattern.)
- **The peace through worship** – Many psalms shift from lament to praise, showing how the psalmists (David among them) moved from pain to peace through honest prayer and choosing to focus on God's character.
- **The discovery that questions don't disqualify relationship** – God called David, "I have found David the son of Jesse, a man after mine own heart, which shall fulfill all my will" (Acts 13:22) despite, or perhaps because of, his honest wrestling with hard realities and circumstances. Within his worship, he found clarity, he found correction, and he found his path.

Strength in Scripture

As I walked through my grief, the Bible became a source of strength and comfort. I found myself turning to the words of the Bible, not out of duty, but due to desperate need. As tears filled my eyes, and I lacked the perfect words to express my "Why," my "How," my "Why now?" or my "When will it end?"; it was only his Word that held the words. There were times I read the verse and couldn't pray, as all I had were groans and tears. These verses took the ache of my heart and placed my pain at the feet of God. I clung to verses that spoke of God's faithfulness, His promises, and His unchanging love. These weren't just words on a page. They became lifelines that anchored me when everything else felt uncertain.

- "Come unto me, all ye that labor and are heavy laden, and I will give you rest." (Matthew 11:28)

- "And God shall wipe away all tears from their eyes; and there shall be no more death, neither sorrow, nor crying, neither shall there be any more pain: for the former things are passed away." (Revelation 21:4)
- "The Lord is my shepherd; I shall not want. He maketh me to lie down in green pastures: he leadeth me beside the still waters. He restoreth my soul: he leadeth me in the paths of righteousness for his name's sake." (Psalm 23:1-3)
- "Blessed be God, even the Father of our Lord Jesus Christ, the Father of mercies, and the God of all comfort. Who comforteth us in all our tribulation, that we may be able to comfort them which are in any trouble, by the comfort wherewith we ourselves are comforted of God." (2 Corinthians 1:3-4)
- "Let not your heart be troubled: ye believe in God, believe also in me. In my Father's house are many mansions: if it were not so, I would have told you. I go to prepare a place for you. And if I go and prepare a place for you, I will come again, and receive you unto myself; that where I am, there ye may be also." (John 14:1-3)
- "It is of the Lord's mercies that we are not consumed, because his compassions fail not. They are new every morning: great is thy faithfulness." (Lamentations 3:22-23)
- "But I would not have you to be ignorant, brethren, concerning them which are asleep, that ye sorrow not, even as others which have no hope For if we believe that Jesus died and rose again, even so them also which sleep in Jesus will God bring with him." (1 Thessalonians 4:13-14)

A Faith That Sustains

Over time, my faith helped me see that my grief wasn't meaningless. While I would never wish for the losses I endured, I began to understand that God could use my pain for a purpose. He used this time to expand my faith in him. What I felt was an indication my faith was bent and warped, was my faith granting me no special permission, no fast pass, nor did it offer escape. Instead, it offered a container large enough to hold both the unbearable pain and the stubborn refutation that this, too, was somehow part of the story.

In grief, we have no choice but to sit comfortably. It is in this discomfort that many often drift from God. The pain of no longer feeling connected to a purpose left me groping for glimpses of hope as a means to reassure my faith. At that moment, my broken faith needed answers. But in the growth, I see that it was my pain that needed answers. A hollow and broken faith was groomed as a result of loss and pain. In this pain, although hard, I clung to the peace I had through His word. I clung to His garment through prayer. I clung to what He could do, His power that I had experienced in His favor before. Grief stripped away the superficial, forcing me to confront the deepest parts of myself and my beliefs. I realized that faith isn't about avoiding pain. It's about trusting God to walk with us through it.

The Apostle Paul's words in 2 Corinthians 12:9 became a mantra for me: "And he said unto me, My grace is sufficient for thee: for my strength is made perfect in weakness. Most gladly therefore will I rather glory in my infirmities, that the power of Christ may rest upon me..." I discovered that God's grace truly was sufficient, sustaining me when I felt I had nothing left to give. My faith in God didn't take away my grief, but it gave me the strength to carry it. It reminded me that even in the depths of pain, I am held by a love that never fails. It taught me that joy and sorrow can coexist, that hope can bloom even in the darkest seasons. Grief changed my relationship with God. In my weakness, I learned to depend on Him in ways I never had before. Prayer was the only place I could bring my rawest emotions and still be held in love.

To you, walking through grief, navigating the new terrain of living without this piece of you that means so much, I offer this encouragement: hold onto faith with everything you have. Even when it feels fragile, even when the questions outnumber the answers, trust that God is with you. He sees your tears, He feels your pain, and He promises to walk with you every step of the way. In the words of Isaiah 41:10: "So do not fear, for I am with you; do not be dismayed, for I am your God. I will strengthen you and help you; I will uphold you with my righteous right hand." My prayers moved from, "God, please take this pain away" to "God, increase my faith and cradle my heart as I lean into this forever-changing space." Faith doesn't remove the pain of grief, but it transforms it. It turns despair into hope, weakness into strength, and loss into purpose. Through faith, I've learned that even in the midst of sorrow, God is faithful, and that is a truth I hold onto with all my heart.

7 Things I Learned About a Faith That Sustains:

1. **Questions Will Cross Your Mind** – Faith doesn't require the absence of questions, and your doubts don't disqualify your faith. Write them down, speak them aloud, and trust that honest questions are the raw material from which deeper faith is forged.
2. **Seek Companions, Not Fixers** – Surround yourself with people who can sit with you in the darkness without trying to turn on the lights prematurely.
3. **Embrace Lament as Prayer:** A lament is the ancient art of bringing your full, unedited anguish before God. This raw honesty is not the opposite of faith—it is faith refusing to lie. Write your own laments, scream them in your car, and trust that reality is sturdy enough to handle your fury.
4. **Find Faith in Small Wonders** – When the big picture makes no sense, zoom in. Notice the small things that restore your faith that God is still good. The morning light, watching children laugh, seeing trees change color in the fall. These tiny moments don't explain suffering, but they remind you that not everything is darkness. Keep a list of these moments, however brief or seemingly insignificant.
5. **Let Your Body Pray** – When words fail, let your body carry your faith. Walk, breathe intentionally, stretch, cry, dance, even if it's just swaying in your living room. Allow your body to carry what your words fail to capture. Your body knows things your mind doesn't, and sometimes it will lead you back to faith when your thoughts cannot.
6. **Revisit Your Story** – Look back at other hard times you've survived. Not to compare suffering, but to remind yourself of your resilience.

How did you make it through that diagnosis, that divorce, that job loss? Nothing but the hand of God. These memories become testimonies, proof that you have survived 100 percent of your worst days so far.

7. **Accept That Faith Will Look Different** – You may not return to the faith you had before. The songs that once moved you might now ring hollow, the theology that made sense might seem inadequate. This isn't failure. It's transformation. This is why there is no timeline or gauge to the length of time given to grief. It takes time. But no matter the time frame, remain in the presence of God.

CHAPTER 5

CHALLENGING MISCONCEPTIONS ABOUT GRIEF

Grief, though universal, is often misunderstood. With faith, I often found myself challenging the societal constraints placed through expectations on how we should grieve, how long it should last, and how it should look. These misconceptions can make an already painful journey even harder, leaving those grieving feeling isolated, judged, or pressured to perform a version of "acceptable" grief.

Understanding and addressing these misconceptions is crucial. Grief doesn't follow a script—it is deeply personal and as unique as the relationships we've lost. In this chapter, we'll explore some of the most common myths about grief, how they impact those who are grieving, and how we can respond with authenticity and self-compassion.

The Scriptures reveal that the timing of God is not our timing and healing occurs in God's time, not man's schedule. We all know too well the scripture in Ecclesiastes that says, "A time to weep and a time to laugh, a time to mourn and a time to dance." Yet what many rush over is the fact that all that is used to describe time itself, not a measure of it or description of duration. It doesn't throw us deadlines or benchmarks for planting, reaping, or sorrow. Rather, it explores the hidden truth that they are unto themselves in terms of timing. It simply acknowledges that each of them should happen, since they are integral to human existence, and in their happening we are to submit to the natural occurrence of their running their course.

As a pastor, I've learned how to fight the temptation to "solve" people's grief or speed up the process. I will be honest and say I didn't feel this way at the start of my journey more than thirty years ago. But as I experienced heartaching grief myself, I began to walk in the shoes that I saw many walk before me, and I understood how insensitive and painful it is to time people in their grief. My job was never to fix anyone instantly but to walk with them down the valley, to remind them that God is with them even in the dark, and to trust that healing awaits and happens in its own time and in its own way.

A perfect example of this is the resurrection story itself, which tells us something about timing in grief. Jesus was in the tomb for three days. He was not there as a semblance of the absence of God, but as a reminder that even divine victories require this visible season of defeat. Grief is our tomb time. It's the space between loss and whatever we may find in new life. Rushing this process isn't faithful to God—it's faithless, as He is working in your tomb time. It's not trusting that something meaningful is going on when we don't see it. The misconceptions of grief, and personifying them, rush past what this experience involves.

> *"Grief is never something you get over. You don't wake up one morning and say, 'I've conquered that: now I'm moving on.' It's something that walks beside you every day. And if you can learn how to manage it and honor the person that you miss, you can take something that is incredibly sad and have some form of positivity."*
>
> —Terri Erwin

Misconception 1: "You Should Get Over It Quickly"

The most prevalent misconception is that grief exists in a predefined schedule. Those close to you often find the right time to ask you if you're "feeling better yet" just weeks or months after a loss, as if grief wears a "timer" around its neck, waiting on the perfect time to be "ready." Discussions are often framed as if the conversation about it should end well after a certain point in time that the person has set in their mind. This can make you feel that you are always "behind the curve" or that you seem "to be taking so long" if you do not return to your normal self.

Many people tend to feel rewarded for "bouncing back" from a few months of going through the motions. Society often applauds those who bounce back quickly but applies heavy pressure on those who need more time to digest their emotions. The widespread expectation for us to move on from grief is probably the most damaging myth about bereavement. This pressure, though well-meaning but ultimately futile, seems to be the common thread of the perception of grief. And the intender is preventing rather than supporting the healing of the intended. Believing that moving on is the same as forgetting is falling into the trap of the fundamentally misguided. It ignores the reality that mourning is not a passing disease to overcome, but also a complex, intrinsically individual process firmly embedded within the very fabric of our lives.

The relentless urge to "move on" or "overcome it" obscures the visceral reality of the grieving process. The implication of such expectations is guilt and shame, creating even more emotional trauma. The idea that grieving has a time frame or that there is a "correct" way to grieve violates the individual nature of the process, and it robs a person of the time that is their due to respond to everything that has happened to them. In fact, the overall urge to make sure that everyone moves on quickly discourages emotions from showing openly and stifles normal expressions of grief. Such triggers can result in the unhealthy coping strategies of avoidance, emotional suppression, or substance abuse. Avoiding responses like this may provide transient coping but will not be the method that facilitates proper processing of a loss, and it does nothing to promote the process of mourning and integrating it within one's life. Realizing that grieving takes time, that there is no such thing as a one-size-fits-all approach, is a key part of any healthy grieving process.

I reflected on why we had such pressure to move on from these feelings. In terms of the past, we have countless notions that long periods of grieving take place, or may take weeks or months, even years, depending on what culture or period of time you live in. Time periods of people who fostered, and in some cases, made those who were grieving themselves sit with his/her feelings rather than hurry the memory of that person or circumstances into the future. But somehow, the clock on the grieving experience has been twisted into a clock of unfathomable time expectations produced by the unknown. We are now at the stage and moment in time where we are left grieving right after the person is laid to rest or the job is gone. This makes it impossible for one to spend time attempting to grapple with and to imagine life in that unspeakable void. I have noticed that the motivation behind the pressure to move on stems from the widespread cultural disapproval of grief, a desire not to feel the anxiety of the emotional pain of loss.

We live in a time in which productivity, positivity, and a single set of standards often take precedence. Grief is something to be carried out quietly, a rarity. When grief reaches the table, it brings sadness, and it is not invited to the cookout. Unfortunately, its inherent sadness, vulnerability, and disruption of routine fit into this frame uneasily. The result is an unexpressed belief that loss must be quelled quickly, that we must immediately transition back into our "normal" lives again, as if the loss never occurred.

In our community, I have seen mothers who lost children to violence being told they must "stay strong for the family" just days after burial. Widows returned to work within a week because financial survival demanded it, while their hearts were still learning how to beat without their partners. The myth of the "strong Black woman" and the "resilient Black man" often leaves no room for the tenderness that grief requires.

James Baldwin, in his profound understanding of human suffering, wrote about the weight of carrying pain that society refuses to acknowledge.[13] While not specifically about grief, his insights into endurance speak to our experience: the way we're expected to bear loss with a kind of superhuman strength, as if our history of survival means we don't need time to heal. But Baldwin also understood that this expectation was another form of violence—denying us our full humanity, including our right to mourn fully and completely.

---

13 Baldwin, J. (1955). *Notes of a Native Son.* Beacon Press.

Jandy Nelson, whose own words have carried so many through loss, spoke of grief as something that "never goes away. It becomes part of you, step for step, breath for breath."[14] Toni Morrison, in her novel *Beloved*, showed us that unprocessed grief becomes a haunting presence, that attempting to move on too quickly from trauma and loss can literally come back to demand our attention.[15] Morrison understood what our ancestors held onto, that grief must be witnessed, held, and honored, not rushed past in service of productivity or others' comfort. This pressure creates a heavy burden on the grievers, who are then left with the looming feelings of not measuring up, or feeling guilty, or even ashamed, of having the most natural and human reaction to grief. And honestly, grieving isn't ever finished. It changes shape and flows like water in a strange vase. Sometimes it's manageable, and sometimes it knocks the wind out of us months, even years, later.

Healing doesn't happen in a linear approach, and no one should feel any need to "choose to move on." The nature of grief changes, but it stays with us because love leaves a long-lasting imprint. So, one of the best ways that I can describe healing is not simply forgetting or suppressing our grief, but accepting our grief, acknowledging it, facing it, allowing it to be a part of the daily life we live, and weaving it into the fabric of our life. Rather than try to "get over" grief, let's learn to carry it. That might mean we'll let ourselves cry at anniversaries, cherish artifacts, and keep a good memory of loved ones alive, or just permit ourselves to feel sadness when it arrives. We do not conquer grieving on this score. Grief is a lifestyle that is assimilated into our hearts and minds.

Misconception 2: "You Have to Be Strong"

Often, in public, there is an unspoken expectation that grieving people should "hold it together." Phrases like "stay strong" or "don't cry" are meant to help people, but they can leave someone feeling like their emotions are a burden. The pressure to be strong causes people to suppress grief, which delays healing. True strength lies not in repressing pain, but in allowing ourselves to experience that pain fully. Tears are not a weakness. They are a

14 Nelson, J. (2010). *The Sky Is Everywhere*. Dial Books.

15 Morrison, T. (1987). *Beloved*. Knopf.

release, a reminder of the depth of our love and loss. Vulnerability is one of the most courageous acts in grief. It's okay to let others see your pain. When people ask how you are doing and your reply is "not well," it's perfectly okay to say so. Grief is messy, and the ability to give yourself permission to grieve authentically is vital, even if it makes others uncomfortable.

When we tell someone to "stay strong in their grief," we believe we are providing encouragement. But what we're doing is more complex and often more harmful. We're telling them their pain is too much for us to witness or that they are taking up more space than they are allowed at this moment. We're asking them to regulate their emotions, not for their own well-being, but for our sake. We're saying that there is a right way and a wrong way to grieve, and the wrong way is crying, anger, despair, or any other totally natural response to loss.

Zora Neale Hurston, who faced her own share of loss and struggle, understood the danger of masking pain as strength. In her work, she showed how communities that expect superhuman strength from their members often create more harm than healing.[16] She knew that when we force people to carry their suffering in silence, it doesn't disappear. Instead, it transforms into toxic tools that entangle the emotional structures that define the person. It becomes depression, addiction, rage, or a kind of walking death where the person is technically alive but no longer truly living.

As I endeavored in my grief experience, I have had to unlearn some things I was taught about strength and faith. I was taught that crying is something you do privately; that in public, one must contain grief and be dignified. But I have come to realize that tears do not do anything against faith. Frequently, tears become the most honest manifestation of what was, the void that is, and the desire of what is to come. True comfort does not remove pain. Instead, it bears witness to it, makes room for it, and reassures the grieving person that they don't have to carry the weight on their own.

I often think about the power of hymns and spirituals. They weren't just songs of strength. They were songs asking God for mercy from the darkest depths of despair and believing that God heard those cries. "Sometimes

---

16 Hurston, Z. N. (1937). *Their Eyes Were Watching God.* J. B. Lippincott & Co.

I Feel Like a Motherless Child," "Nobody Knows the Trouble I've Seen," "Precious Lord, Take My Hand"—these are songs of vulnerability, covered in tears and invoking compassion. In that vulnerability, our ancestors discovered not weakness but connection to God and each other, to their own humanity. Genuine strength in grieving doesn't resemble the strength most people associate with it. Strength in grief is not without tears. Strength in grief is the bravery to let the tears fall. It's not keeping it all together, but it's letting yourself fall apart with trusted people who are there to help you piece some parts back together. It's not walking through loss unbothered, but it's allowing loss to transform you and the confidence that who you are on the other side can still be beautiful and whole, even if it's different.

Audre Lorde, who approached her own mortality with rare bravery, recognized this difference. "Caring for myself is not self-indulgence, it is self-preservation," she wrote.[17] Allowing ourselves to grieve completely and feel our pain completely but also be very exposed in our loss is the sort of radical self-preservation that respects our love as well as our humanity. I've watched people who tried to be strong through their grief or given in when they couldn't help but be broken. And those who want to be strong are usually brittle, fragile in ways they never meant to be fragile. They're way too happy to smile a lot, work too much, or shut down emotionally. The ones who give in to breaking, who can feel their pain intensely and allow others to share and see it, find a power even more incredible, a strength they didn't even know they had. Not the strength of the oak that doesn't bend and ends up broken, but the strength of the willow that bends with the gust and survives in such a tempest.

We serve a God who was strong enough to become weak, powerful enough to become vulnerable, divine enough to become human and to suffer and to die. If strength was simply about being unaffected by pain, then the cross would be meaningless. But the cross teaches us that sometimes the most powerful thing you can do is allow yourself to be broken, to feel everything, to trust that love is worth the cost, even when the cost feels unbearable. In grief, we don't need to be strong. We need to be real, to be honest, to be

---

17 Lorde, A. (1988). *A Burst of Light: Essays.* Firebrand Books.

held. We need to trust that our brokenness is not the end of our story but perhaps the place where our most authentic story finally begins to be told.

In my experience, one of the most important things I had to give myself permission to do was to come apart. I gave myself permission to cry when I heard my mother's favorite hymn. I told myself that it's okay to get teary-eyed at the sight of my father's smile. It was okay to need help with things I couldn't verbalize. I remember thinking, *Clive, it's okay to not be okay.* The permission I held onto for so long out of fear that I wasn't processing their loss correctly, or that I wasn't being strong in light of being afraid. This permission is particularly essential for people who have devoted their lives to being strong for others. The mother who held her family together through crisis after crisis, the father who never was weak, the eldest child who must always lead by example. These are people who do not know how to receive care, how to be fragile, or how to appear as anything other than put together. But grief requires us to learn. It shows our pretenses and demands that we recognize our deep-seated need to connect, to be held, and that we want to belong and have a community.

Navigating Well-Meaning but Hurtful Comments

One of the most difficult aspects of grieving is dealing with the words and comments of good hearted but clueless people who do not completely appreciate your pain. Statements like "Everything happens for a reason" or "They're in a better place now" can seem dismissive, even when they are meant to soothe. Other comments, like, "You can have the time to rest now" after job loss or "At least you had time to say goodbye" when a person passes, can inadvertently trivialize your suffering. These statements usually arise from a place of discomfort, and the person who made them doesn't know what to say. This is why they try to grab words that feel reassuring but leave you feeling more broken than before. When faced with such comments, you don't have to educate or rationalize your grief. You can reply with kindness and still preserve your space and boundaries. I remember after hearing these words myself, I said, "I know you mean well, but that's not helpful right now." After my voice came back and a friend told me that I should just be thankful I still have a voice and not to dwell on the past, I had to let them know, "I appreciate your concern, but I just need someone to listen."

It's fine, too, to let the comment pass behind you, to prioritize what you need over how someone else responds, but boundaries are essential to the process because words matter in loss and grief. Over time I have observed the strange pattern where people who would never dream of providing medical advice to a patient feel uniquely qualified to give emotional solutions to grief. Standing at gravesides, sitting in hospital waiting rooms, moving across the receiving lines at homegoing services, the words fly without thought, boundary, or regard. I have heard the array of phrases people offer when confronted with someone else's raw pain. The irony is that those who mean the most harm often say the least, while those who mean the most good can inflict wounds that last longer than the original loss. It's a painful reminder that good intentions minus wisdom can prove just another burden for those grieving.

In his great work *Invisible Man*, Ralph Ellison found our society reacts to pain it won't see or comprehend. He wrote, "I am invisible, understand, simply because people refuse to see me." The grieving person often faces this very invisibility, not because someone says nothing, but because they will never see their pain at its true depth, the intricacies of their losses, the truth that sometimes wounds don't heal based on others' timelines or expectations. When someone reassures a grieving parent, "God needed another angel," they are not talking about the mother who will never hear her child laughing again, the father who will never be able to teach his son to drive, the siblings who will be raised with an empty space at every holiday table. They are reductions of a complex, elaborate human being to a simplistic saying, providing an inexcusable explanation to something that can no longer be explained.

The patterns of these well-meaning but damaging comments fall into unique categories that are well known. These comments attempt to minimize pain by suggesting it could be worse. They operate on the flawed premise that grief can be measured and that some losses are more acceptable than others. These comments suggest that what we've lost can be substituted, that love is interchangeable, that relationships are replaceable commodities rather than irreplaceable connections. While growth and service may indeed emerge from loss, prescribing these outcomes to someone in fresh grief is like telling someone with a broken leg that they'll appreciate walking more once it heals.

The goal is not to become unyielding or to avoid others' attempts to comfort or console you. The goal is to learn when a person's voice deserves to be heard and when it does not—and the result is that you may listen more or less with caution when someone tries to speak with compassion about your grief while still keeping a good distance from it. Ultimately, negotiating hurtful comments during mourning is learning to value your own wisdom over others' discomfort, not to sacrifice self to others' desire for convenience, and to remember that whoever has been given permission to talk into your pain is also usually the one who can stand silently with it. The words that heal are not the words that explain your pain. They are the words that honor it, hold space for it, and say you are not walking this road alone. Those are the voices that are worth hearing. The rest of it, as many other literary works instruct us, can be granted grace and then gently shelved so you can press forward on your essential path toward whatever wholeness awaits you on the other side of loss.

Advocating for Your Needs During Grief

Grief is hard, physically and emotionally. To work it out, you've got to keep your own well-being at the forefront, even if it's setting boundaries or asking for help. Yes, I understand that advocating for your needs may feel uncomfortable at first, particularly if you're accustomed to putting other people ahead of yourself, but doing so is a vital step in the healing process. Grief is an essential paradox because we desperately need connection but also experience loneliness in the struggle to mourn. Others might find it hard to grasp how deep the experience of your loss really goes and how unscripted your healing is. Your good-hearted friends might say things like, "Try some deep breathing or something," or your family members might pressure you to follow a timeline that may not coincide with your internal rhythms.

For me, my condition had taken away my ability to speak, but not having the words to speak up for myself catapulted me back to when I lost my parents. Yes, I had experienced loss before and would experience it again soon after with my brothers, but the gut wrenching reality of loss hit me differently having to say farewell to them. My condition had already paralyzed my voice, but the fear of not having the words I needed to advocate for myself was an all-to-familiar one. I felt the same way when my parents died.

As I worked through my emotional plight, I truly felt the pain of my recovery worsened when the feeling of helplessness became almost an everyday experience because I couldn't speak. I became angrier, not with the situation, but the way it reminded me of a pain that I had worked so hard to suppress. The weariness of the loss can cause emotion so draining that it's hard to even know that you want to know what you want, let alone say it to other people properly. You might feel like a burden, you might be afraid that people will distance themselves from you if you are too candid about your troubles, or you might just be too drowsy to ever have any serious discussions. Establishing your advocacy voice amid grief begins by attuning to your inner landscape.

I had to take the time to distinguish what was supportive and what was draining. Not everything that was well intended was well received. I learned the necessary art of monitoring what interactions made me feel heard and which ones left me feeling more alone. Sometimes your body may speak for you in how you want to handle it—the clenching of your shoulders, for instance, means that someone is not following your instructions, while tears can come from a helpful presence and sense of safety. Your needs in mourning will change and evolve as time passes. What's helpful during the onset of grief can feel intrusive months down the line and support you resisted initially may feel useful to you as you heal.

You must realize this and change what and where you stand in life and what you want. For example, you can have more specific follow-up conversations with people who want to help: "I know I said I needed space before, but now I'm finding that I really need a little bit more connection." Or "This process of checking in isn't working for me anymore—could we try something different?" You are not wrong for growing, and you are not wrong for changing your mind. You are entitled to adjust your boundaries.

Eventually, having your needs fulfilled in grief is a matter of finding a steady rhythm that respects both the continued process of healing and your role within society. This is not about selfishness or demands. This is about clarity. Once you understand what you need and are able to set boundaries, you are far more available for real connections. Your grief is teaching you something you need to know—to recognize your current needs, values, and limits. We navigate the day-to-day, being respectful of other peoples' boundaries, and often being willing to bend our own to fit what they need. Then, when the time comes for us to respect our own, we lack the tools to communicate them clearly. Speaking out in these moments, or for me, writing them out, isn't just about bearing your loss. It's to include the knowledge that grieving pushes you to live on, even though there has been loss.

The skills it teaches you about being able to advocate for yourself when you're in this vulnerable phase of grief will help you with your ability to have stronger, deeper relationships. In demanding your needs while grieving, you are not only providing for your own needs, you're showing others that we can love one another in grief in calm and gentle ways that preserve the dignity of the griever. This is just one of the deepest gifts you can give to your community: an invitation to help in meaningful ways.

Here are some ways to advocate for yourself during grief:

- **Ask for Space When You Need It**
    - When feeling overwhelmed by social interactions or obligations, it's okay to say no. "No" is a complete sentence. Grief, in all its stages, requires solitude at times. It is an opportunity to sit with your emotions without distractions. Too often we place ourselves in social settings owing to the fear of disappointing others and leave ourselves exposed prematurely. There are times that you will have to step away from social interactions, family gatherings, or just well-meaning check-ins to reflect on the loss and how you feel in private. This isn't antisocial behavior. It's setting healthy boundaries that allow your mind and heart to

do the work of healing. Let others know when you need space and reassure them it's not personal, it's part of your process.

- Be straightforward and have clear boundaries about your availability. Don't hint or expect people to just know—make plain to them exactly what you need. Vague statements, like "I need a bit of time," are open to misunderstanding and continued interruptions. Instead, be clear about timeframes and what space looks like for you. "I need three days with no visitors or phone calls. I'll reach out on Friday to let you know how I'm doing." Or: "I'm not ready for social visits yet, but I appreciate texts that don't require responses." Or: "I need to skip family dinner this Sunday and probably the next few Sundays. I'll let you know when I'm ready to join again."
- Remember that asking for space doesn't mean you lack gratitude for support or that you are driving people away forever. You're just saying that healing involves both connection and solitude, and at this moment, you need the solitude part.

- **Express What You Need from Others**
  - People often want to help but don't know how. Be honest about what you need. If you need someone to sit with you in silence, say so. Most people will be grateful for the clarity and eager to support you.
  - Be specific about what you need. The biggest error among grieving people is to say, "I'm fine" when you're drowning, or to ask for "help" without being clear what that help needs to look like. Your loved ones genuinely want to support you, but for many of them, grief is a foreign concept. They need your guidance to help effectively. Instead of saying meals are a struggle, say, "I need someone to bring dinner on Tuesdays and Fridays for the next month." Instead of "I need support," just say, "I need someone to call me every morning just to check in, not to fix anything, just to remind me I'm not alone."

- Rather than, "I don't know what I need," try "I need someone to sit with me in silence for an hour," or "I need help with grocery shopping because I can't handle the crowds right now."
- Consider building a network in which various players have to offer different things. You might have a practical helper who's good at organizing, cooking, or managing logistics. The listener who can hear your stories without trying to fix anything. Not everybody can provide all kinds of support. Your mother could be a master at practical things but struggle with emotional support. Your best friend may be a great listener but terrible at organizing. This is normal and okay. Use different people for different needs rather than expecting one person to be everything. Consider making a support schedule that matches people's strengths to your needs over time.

- **Set Boundaries Around Well-Meaning Advice**
  - Maintaining a good boundary in grief entails clarity and reliability. This could involve telling people straight up what you need: "Right now, I need people to listen without trying to fix or explain my grief." It might be about cutting back on the time spent with some family members who always give you unhelpful advice.
  - One approach might be to have friends check in with you before giving suggestions for how you should be reacting. Another way to use boundary setting is switching the subject if someone talks about grief in a way that seems invasive or unhelpful. At times it means leaving a gathering early when the conversations become an exercise in unwanted advice about your healing process.
  - Sometimes that means being direct. If someone is pushing you to "move on" or handle your grief a certain way, it's okay to set boundaries. You might say, "I know you're trying to help, but I need to grieve in my own way." Boundaries aren't walls. They're gates, just as you are the gatekeeper. You determine what goes in and out, and the times doing them feels good to you and is

conducive to your recovery. Survival and eventual healing are your mission in grief, and anything that interferes with that mission needs to be handled or ruled out.

- **Prioritize Self-Care**
    - Grief often depletes your energy, so it's important to nurture yourself. Whether it's taking a walk, journaling, or simply resting, self-care is not selfish—it's necessary.
    - Self-care in times of mourning does not need to be elaborate or time-consuming. It may be taking a walk in nature when you need to move stagnant energy or simply writing down your feelings when emotions feel overwhelming.
    - The secret is to listen to what your body, mind, and spirit need in each moment and honor those needs without judgment. And keep in mind that taking care of yourself during grief is not selfish. It is actually one of the most loving things you can do, both for yourself and for those who care about you.
    - And when you're prioritizing your well-being, you're creating the foundation necessary to navigate grief with greater resilience and to gradually rebuild your strength for the journey ahead.

Breaking the Myths of Grief

Challenging such misconceptions starts with redefining grief. It's wild, it's unpredictable, and deeply personal. It isn't neatly layered or timeline-driven. It does not require that we be "strong," as society has so often defined strength. The Bible bears to rest the understanding of grief as deep and ongoing.

When King David wept and fasted for seven days during the death of his infant son, he was then able to bring himself to worship the Lord for the life of his child. Later, when his adult son Absalom rebelled against him, David's grief so filled him that it triumphed over his military victory: "And the king was much moved, and went up to the chamber over the gate, and wept: and as he went, thus he said, O my son Absalom, my son, my son Absalom! would God I had died for thee, O Absalom, my son, my son!" (2

Samuel 18:33) Two distinct losses, yet two completely different expressions of grief from the same person, neither incorrect, both true to the relationship and situation. The psalms may provide the starkest observations on the unpredictable nature of grief, while also honoring the stages and the missed opportunity of confining it to look a certain way. David explains in Psalm 42:3: "My tears have been my meat day and night, while they continually say unto me, Where is thy God?" yet in Psalm 30:5, "For his anger endureth but a moment; in his favor is life: weeping may endure for a night, but joy cometh in the morning." These are not contradictory statements but a recognition that grief flows like an unpredictable tide.

Of course, the obsession with "moving on" in modern life leads to an unbalanced experience with grief, creating a kind of fantasy timetable that bears little resemblance to our heart's ability to love and feel pain. Lewis tells and confirms that there is no map. Grief doesn't care about our timelines and the convenience of our social relationships and expectations. "Grief isn't a checklist" to move on from, but rather an opportunity to engage with the hard truths that our emotions strive to teach us.

C. S. Lewis, in *A Grief Observed*, says:

> ...a totally new landscape. As I've already noted, not every bend does. Sometimes the surprise is the opposite one; you are presented with exactly the same sort of country you thought you had left behind miles ago. That is when you wonder whether the valley isn't a circular trench. But it isn't. There are partial recurrences, but the sequence doesn't repeat.[18]

It reflects the Biblical mandate to bear one another's burdens. Paul says, "Bear ye one another's burdens, and so fulfill the law of Christ." (Galatians 6:2) Remember, he doesn't say "fix each other's burdens" or "eliminate each other's burdens," but carry them. This suggests presence, endurance, and shared weight rather than quick fixes. The book of Job can possibly offer scripture's most extensive examination of how we should not support someone in grieving. Job's friends showed up with good intentions, sitting alone with him for seven days, their most helpful act. But when they start talk-

18 Lewis, C. S. (1961). *A Grief Observed.* HarperOne.

ing, they make a rush to explain, justify, or seek repair for his misery. They cannot simply stand there in mystery and pain. Job's response is honest, necessary, yet often characterized as harsh. "I have heard many such things: miserable comforters are ye all!" (Job 16:2)

When society tells a person that their grief is "too much" or "too long," we run the risk of becoming Job's friends. Fleetingly offering miserable comfort rather than authentic presence. From my experience, I learned that one of the most valid things that can be offered in moments of grief is your presence. Not a struggle to have the right words, or the right tone, just arms and a heart wide open—doing more, being more, loving more.

Maya Angelou, in her work *I Know Why the Caged Bird Sings,* said: "There is no greater agony than having an untold story inside you."[19] In my moments of thinking about my parents, those around me, things I have loved and lost, I learned that grief is not something to fix, to rush through, or to suppress. It is something to be lived, felt, and shared, with the understanding that we have to let go of what we thought it should be to live what it could be. And in doing so, we honor both the depth of our pain and the enduring power of our love. Grief becomes healing when it turns into a story, when it moves from isolation to being witnessed, from silence to sacred sharing. Klass, Silverman, and Nickman shed light on an important bereavement concept in the book *Continuing Bonds: New Understandings of Grief.* They explain that the idea of "continuing bonds" is an understanding that real grieving doesn't require "letting go" or "moving on" but finding new ways to stay connected with those we've lost.

Paul writes in his letter to the Thessalonians, in 1 Thessalonians 4:13, "But I would not have you to be ignorant, brethren, concerning them which are asleep, that ye sorrow not, even as others which have no hope." He's not telling them not to grieve, but he's telling them to grieve with hope and in love, understanding that death is not the final word. When we avoid cultural pressure to "get over it" or "find closure," we move to a place where, instead of excluding, we embrace. Establishing places where people weep,

---

19 Angelou, M. (1969). *I Know Why the Caged Bird Sings*. New York, NY: Random House.

where mentioning a loved one that has gone on doesn't create stillness and anniversary dates are not ignored but celebrated.

It is a reflection of Jesus' promise: "Blessed are they that mourn: for they shall be comforted." (Matthew 5:4) Because the comfort lies not in refusing to mourn, but in a community that has sorrow and hope to share. If we challenge these myths, both as grievers, and as a community, then we make a place for grief to be what grief has always been: love, in its most vulnerable form, the price and privilege of having loved someone deeply. In paying homage to our grief, we pay homage to our ability to love. And it is not about wallowing in sorrow or rejecting hope. It is about creating space for the whole range of the human experience of loss to unravel. All while having faith that our hearts are big enough to carry both immense tragedy and love that endures. There, we may find healing, not as an end or a means to an end, but as a journey, not the absence of pain because community is there, demystifying myths, and bearing witness to life in a newly blossomed form.

CHAPTER 6

STORIES OF RESILIENCE

Grief takes so many forms, and losing my voice was a grief I just hadn't foreseen. It taught me that even short-lasting losses can cut deep and lead us to face facets of ourselves that we would rather slip under the radar, but it also taught me resilience. My voice, my true voice, is more than a sound, and I learned that it mattered more than that. It's the way I show love, the bond I have with others, and the way I live authentically, even in the face of silence. This taught me that grief is not contained to just the feelings involved in losing the physicality of a person, but it extends to losing parts of you, the things that make up our characteristics, our personalities, and our everyday.

That memory of those ten days stays with me, not as a wound, but as a reminder of the strength that comes from surrendering to the process of healing. In that silence, I not only discovered my voice once more, but also a deeper understanding of who I am and the God who walks with me through every loss, every silence, and every grief. Grief may appear very different for each one of us, yet buried within it lies tales of extraordinary endurance. In my life as a pastor, teacher, and psychologist, I have come across not only my own suffering but also the grieving journeys of many people. Through these experiences, I found evidence that even in our darkest moments, we can still find a way to heal and carry grief with us as we work on reimagined versions of ourselves.

Society tends to mistake resilience for going back to the person we were before the loss hit. We talk about bypassing the experience of the pain and the grief as if grief were a detour in our real lives. But all those who have walked through the valley of profound loss know that this is impossible. The death of a loved one creates a before and after that can never be undone. Resilience, then, is not about erasing this divide but about learning to inhabit the after with purpose and grace. It is the delicate, quiet, gradual, laborious task of building a new life from the ground up around an absence. This reconstruction doesn't come in the big, dramatic bursts we might imagine. It comes in the series of small adjustments we make over time: learning how to cook for just one, sleeping alone without feeling swallowed by the bed's vastness, and coming up with new rituals for holidays that were once shared experiences. The resilient griever doesn't move past these challenges once and run away. Instead, they create rhythms, emotional, practical, and spiritual, that allow them to weather the cycles of loss that will last their whole lives. They know that grief has seasons, and they prepare accordingly.

In writing this, I thought of the number of families I have coached, people and couples. I have helped them to redefine their identity or their marriage, and they have called me to think and ponder on the pain and the power of progress in grief. I say progress not because a person or people are able to move on, but because a person is able to find small glimpses of happiness again, and they are better able to navigate the pains of the process. The "silver lining" for Lewis wasn't happiness returning but a more authentic spiritual life emerging from the wreckage. He learns to hold contradictory truths together and allow them to walk side by side in his day-to-day. This shows that joy is both fleeting and somehow still present, that love persists even when the object of that love is absent, that grief itself becomes a form of connection to what was lost, while building onto what is still here.

I will introduce you to Emma, James, and Maya. Each of them faced the kind of loss that shakes a person to their core, but through their journeys, they discovered strength they didn't know they possessed. Their stories remind us that while grief is deeply personal, its transformative power is universal.

Emma's Journey: Rising from the Depths

When Emma lost her two children in a tragic accident, the world became a hollow, empty place. Her children were her main reason for living. They were the apples of her eye, and most of all, her reason to keep holding on. She took them to school every morning, made them meals to fill their bellies and help them grow big and strong. Her work ethic was built on the foundation of her children. They needed a roof over their heads and a place to sleep at night, so it was no wonder that she excelled at her job. It wasn't just about the salary or the title but making sure that they saw their mother as their hero, a woman who was dedicated to her work, while also being dedicated to her family.

All of this changed one Thursday afternoon. It was supposed to be a fun trip for the kids. It was supposed to be their break for the summer before going back to school in the fall. One call rocked her world, left her with a pitted pain in her stomach more excruciating than anything she could have ever imagined. That call took her breath away. She described those first months as a blur of numbness and tears. "I couldn't imagine how I could ever move forward," she said. "Everything I loved, everything that gave my life meaning, was gone."

In those early days, grief left her paralyzed. She spent hours staring out the window, replaying the moments she could no longer change. Her pain was raw and all-consuming. In all honesty, she admitted the thought of leaving this world crossed her mind more than once, the urge to go be with her children overwhelming in its intensity. The thought of living without them was futile, especially when the emptiness of her home surrounded her. Even worse, when she went into their room and looked around, she couldn't help but hear their laughter and see them tucked into their little beds—it was too much for her, the weight too heavy. The thought that there would come a day that she could be herself again seemed like a distant fantasy. One that would never be her truth.

She questioned why she was given these blessings just to have them snatched from her so viciously, with no warning. Friends and family tried to reach her, but she often pushed them away. She didn't have the energy to explain her sadness or listen to their well-meaning but often misplaced words of comfort. Condolences never truly meant anything and meant even less when people offered them just because they knew of nothing else to say. There was no perfect grief cycle to follow. In all honesty, she hesitated to even call it loss or grieving. Speaking the words would make it all real, would force her to come to terms with the pain of absence, the pain of living without them, and the disruption of seeking support.

During her group therapy sessions a year after their passing, she was finally able to say, for the first time, that her children were gone. Saying that they had passed was something she could never actually formulate the words to describe. The words were too painful, the thought aching, but after constant conversation, she grew the confidence to say these heavy words. After the anger, the aching depression, and the spiraling sadness, she began to journal, writing letters to her children about how she missed them and how she hoped they were well in Heaven. She wrote to her daughter about her toys. Telling her that although she'd packed up her favorite dolls for donation, it wasn't because she was trying to forget about her, but that she had remembered her passion to help other little girls who were less fortunate. The act gave Emma closure, and it began to ease a part of her that she had rendered unmendable. These small acts gave her hope that she would be able to live on with her children in her heart, that grieving was part of the love she had for them.

This sense of hope grew greater when Emma began volunteering at a local shelter for children in crisis. At first, she wasn't sure if she could handle being around kids, afraid it would deepen her pain. But instead, it reminded her of her love for her children and her desire to honor them. "It was like planting seeds in the middle of a wasteland," she explained. "Slowly, new life began to grow in me." The shelter gave her purpose again. She started to connect with the children, helping them feel safe and seen. In giving to others, Emma found a way to process parts of her grief that she failed to put into words. Her healing didn't erase the pain of her loss, but it gave her the strength to carry it. "Grief is still with me," she says, "but so is the love. I've learned they can exist side by side."

James's Healing: Finding Community in Loneliness

When James arrived at his job one Wednesday, it was like every other Wednesday. He grabbed his coffee at the thirty-third-floor kitchen and made his way up the elevator to his office on the thirty-fourth. He walked into his office, and not too long after getting settled in his chair, he heard a tap at the door. It was his manager, who told him, "Come to my office when you get a chance." His tone was average, though James could tell something was off about his greeting. He didn't stop to talk about the basketball game the night before, or how his favorite team wasn't looking too hopeful in making the championship this year. James just thought that his manager had a busy morning, but when he arrived at his manager's office, he saw the head of HR sitting in the office as well. The words came across with a chilled, emotionless tone: "James, we have valued you and your work, but due to company cuts, we have to let you go." All other words shared in this moment dissipated like clouds in the midday sky.

Before he returned to his desk, his things were already packed, the past twenty years of his life now boxed into a one-sentence dismissal. Before he could even think about what he would do, where he would go, security was at the door to escort him out of the building, like some thieving criminal. He returned to his car, and tears welled in his eyes. He screamed in anger and defeat, the dismissal, the years of commitment, the emotionless, relentless drain of his time and energy. He began to spiral as the thoughts raged through his head.

He found himself feeling confused and broken over the next couple of days. He even got dressed the following morning out of habit, and then it hit him that he no longer had a job to report to. His body had held onto a routine, and releasing this muscle memory would take more time than he could think of in the first few weeks. He questioned God, questioned himself and his future, and he questioned the practicality of his being able to make ends meet in the meantime. He continued in this cycle of denial for weeks. The despair of what had become his day made it impossible to ask for help, to admit to his family and friends that he was unemployed, and to confront the void that now filled his day, his heart, and his mind. He soon found himself unable to get out of bed, wearing the same clothes, skipping daily grooming essentials, all because they reminded him of his routine that was no longer needed. Depression consumed him and took away any glimpse of light that once existed in his spirit.

Three months into being at home, even deeper into his feelings than he had felt before, James sat in his living room scrolling through his phone when he saw a post from a church member about the men's ministry meeting. Something in him moved that hadn't in months. Maybe it was desperation, maybe it was God speaking to him, but either way, he found himself getting in the shower for the first time in days.

When he arrived, he was surprised at how welcoming the men were. Church was a place he had not been able to attend often because of his work schedule. Usually "Bedside Baptist" was his go-to, and he would listen while he reviewed reports, but coincidentally, he felt like he was meant to be in this very spot on that day.

As the meeting started, he realized that he was not the only one carrying a weight that he could not shake. He recognized the same hollow look he'd been seeing in the mirror in the eyes of some of the other men. It was grief and pain. As they went around the room and shared what it was that brought them out, he heard the same all-too-familiar words. It was the familiar job loss, the shame, the inability to tell his wife how bad things really were. To his surprise, no one looked away. They nodded. They understood. Another man added, "Divorce took everything. The things I thought would never go, my kids, my house, my sense of who I was—gone."

For the first time since that Wednesday, James didn't feel alone.

James kept coming back. Week after week, the meetings became his anchor. He felt the heaviness still, but when he was there, it didn't feel as heavy. His depression didn't feel as consuming, and he felt the permission he always needed to breathe lighter. As time passed, he shared more, hoped more, and felt loved more. And slowly, an idea took root, faith was enlightened, and hope for a brighter tomorrow was reignited. These men needed more than a weekly meeting. They needed ongoing support, professional guidance, and permission to be vulnerable in a world that told them to "man up." James prayed for God to lead, to redirect his path.

He returned to his first love, mentorship. He used his severance to get certified as a peer support specialist and had partnered with two licensed male therapists who donated their time. Six months later, James stood before a group of twenty men and led a program that was in his heart. "Welcome to the first session of Man Talk," James began, his voice steady but full of emotion. "This is a space where we don't have to pretend we've got it all together. Where losing your job doesn't make you less of a man. And where admitting that you're struggling is the bravest thing you can do."

This was the first and only program that was intended. They brought in male mental health counselors who specialized in men's issues for the main session covering depression, anxiety, identity crisis, and transition. They covered practical topics in the workshops like resume building, financial planning during unemployment, and how to talk to your family about struggle. But mostly, they talked. Really talked. James watched men arrive broken and leave with something he recognized—not happiness, but hope and purpose.

On the anniversary of his termination, James stood in that same parking garage where he'd screamed in his car a year earlier. But today, he was heading to his office. A small space above a coffee shop where "Man Talk Foundation" was painted on the door. One evening, a younger man approached him after a session. "I was about to end it all," he said quietly. "Then I found this group. You saved my life." James's eyes filled with tears, but this time they weren't tears of defeat. "No," he said, gripping the man's shoulder. "We saved each other."

Maya's Reflection: Strength in Legacy

The minute Maya heard "cancer" for the first time, everything about who she was leaned on its head. Her father, who had taught her to ride a bike and who called every Sunday just to see how she was doing in her week, suddenly had an expiration date hanging over their conversations. For the next nine months, Maya navigated a space she had never known before, going from daughter to caretaker. Oncology waiting rooms began to resemble her own living room, as she spent more time there than in her own space. She memorized pill names and frequencies, translated medical terms, and became a consistent presence when treatments made him too weak to lift his head up. She saw him shrink, not only in the size of his body, but from the giant she had always seen as invincible, to now needing help with the smallest of tasks.

The thoughts of him humming jazz and the blues while shaving, the ways he insisted on making his own coffee, even with shaky hands, this became her world. When her father died on a Tuesday morning in March, Maya was holding his hand. She said she loved him, that she would be okay, that he had been the best father she had known, and with one last breath, he was gone. Losing her father to cancer shook Maya. As she wept in the telling of her story, she said he was her rock, her guide, the most important source of support in her life. He was the person she turned to whenever life got tough. And then he was gone, and she felt like her compass had gone.

Maya wrestled with anger and guilt for weeks. She was furious that God seemed to take him before he'd had the chance to live out all he wanted, and she felt guilty that she couldn't do more for him in his last months. The "well wishes" led to her lashing out. One friend had told her, "I'm sure he will watch over you forever." The words were well intended, yet dismissive to her reality that she didn't want him to be looking from above, she wanted him to be with her hand in hand. Weeks one and two after his passing were filled with such an odd mixture of numbness and hypersensitivity that she had no idea how to navigate them. She could deal with funeral arrangements but would become emotional seeing his favorite cereal at a grocery store.

Maya wouldn't start to feel a comfortable presence until she started combing through his stuff. As hard as it was, she knew she could not avoid his room and his things forever. Her aunt had tried to help her go through his things before, but she wasn't ready. It was too unreal, too fresh, still too painful. She found an old diary of his, and it was full of thoughts and suggestions of future dreams. An entry, from months before his diagnosis, read: "Maya called today about her promotion. I could hear the passion in her voice, like the sound of excitement, and I remembered at seven she announced that she was going to 'help all the people who don't have homes.'" Although she didn't see it at the time, that was growth for her, embracing her father's memory, while reimagining what life could look like carrying him on in her heart and mind. To her, he wasn't dead and gone. His wisdom and love were still there, threaded through those pages, and woven into where she saw herself and the things she saw to be possible.

The daily phone calls from friends were all gone, the check-ins and popups had slowed down, yet Maya took his words as a guiding light and decided to keep up with his footsteps for her lifelong learning. She used these words as a tool to not lose sight of her daily passions, her daily work. When she found herself being a support to another who was grieving, she realized that being part of a community for someone does not equate to moving on and being above the moment. It is a reality of living with the love of the person and thereby helping others in your community grow. When she spoke for families operating with insurance companies, she tapped into the voice he had taught her to find. The excruciating pain had begun to subsume itself in something that was finally safe, a kind of persistent pain that would flare up for big milestones in her life, only to no longer be as severe as it had been trying to be. Maya also discovered that to heal was not for her to forget or "overcome" the loss. Instead, it meant learning to hold onto her love for her father in new ways.

In a visit to her father's grave, she shared with him, "You showed me how to love well, how to fight for what is right, and how to find meaning in the worst moments." Maya learned that love does not die with the body. Her love for her father fueled her and gave her the ability to rebrand herself. Though her father's death silenced the Earth story that they shared, it didn't stop his influence in her life. By mastering how to live with her dad without his very existence, Maya found ways of having him be a guide with whom she could walk.

The Threads That Connect

The threads that connect these stories are not immediately visible, yet they weave together a tapestry of profound truth. We see that grief is not a singular experience but a multifaceted journey that reveals our deepest vulnerabilities and our most extraordinary strengths. What follows, then, is not a prescription for how to grieve correctly, but a witness to how grief transforms us, shapes our relationships, and ultimately, teaches us what it means to be fully, courageously human.

As I read these stories, I understand that everyone has encountered an Emma, James, or Maya at some time. The details may be slightly different, but the experience threads the same lines. The people in these stories did not choose their loss, yet within their pain, they discovered unexpected restorations, deeper compassion, fierce resilience, and a profound appreciation for life's fragility. Through their stories and mine, I found that healing does not mean forgetting, and that navigating the perils of grief requires us to be tender with ourselves in ways we would never have imagined necessary. Our experiences lighten a path that cannot be written in advance, only recognized in hindsight. And when we look back and realize how far we've traveled from that first moment when everything changed, we can truly say, "To God be the glory!"

The Beginning of New Beginnings:

Each story I shared started out with a fundamental breakdown of self. Emma had lost her position as a mother, the structure upon which she had built a life. James had lost his sense of confidence, and his sense of worth—twin pillars of identity crumbling before his eyes. Maya lost her compass, the father who had steered her to a clear course. I lost my voice, which was the means by which I demonstrated love (or offered guidance) and fulfilled my purpose to the church, as a pastor and teacher.

In all cases, grief demanded a response to an impossible question: Who am I now?

Emma was no longer the mother who packed school lunches and tucked children into bed. James was neither the devoted employee nor the husband who had any more evening chats. Maya was no longer the daughter who talked to her father every Sunday. And I had shifted from the voice that had advised, who had consoled, who had ruled. This thread is among the most disorienting in grief—it doesn't just steal something from us. It threatens our very identity. The person we were before this loss cannot leave their previous life. That version has been irrevocably changed.

Allow the Stillness to Move You to New Places

Another thread running throughout is the period of "stillness," of being imprisoned immediately in the context of loss. For hours Emma sat staring out windows, paralyzed by the absence. James couldn't leave his house, swallowed in the pain that was his loss of identity. Maya went through funeral arrangements in a fog of numbness, then broke down at the sight of her father's favorite cereal. And there I am, unable to speak, forced into a silence that seemed simultaneously claustrophobic and, in a more paradoxical way, essential.

This paralysis is not weakness. It is the mind and body's instinctive response to tremendous loss. We see this in all four stories: an age when advancing seems impossible, a place where the gulf between before and after appears too wide to fill. It is during this time that grief does its most important work. Instead of passively enduring this pain, it confronts us with the enormity of what has been lost, its necessity for us to stop, feel, and comprehend what has been lost. They misread this stillness as getting stuck, but these stories show it to be a necessary state. Emma would not be able to immediately write her first letter to her children. First, she needed those months of staring out the window. Maya needed time before opening her father's diary. And those ten days of enforced silence were needed before I could decipher what my voice actually meant.

Trust the Small Acts That Rebuild

Perhaps the most powerful thread linking these narratives is the idea that healing never arrives in bold and sweeping ways, but in the little acts, as though they were almost imperceptible, of rebuilding. For Emma, it started with writing letters to her kids. These small messages, not full essays, were notes from the heart to express the instant desire to speak to them.

For James, it began, for instance, merely by attending one of the men's ministry meetings. Then he took more steps by being willing to lead devotion. Then starting the Men Talk series. Each act was a small, manageable step, building on the one before.

To Maya, healing started with opening her father's diary, reading one entry, then another. She took his words about her seven-year-old self wanting to "help all the people who don't have homes" and let them inspire her in doing advocacy work that honored his memory.

And as for me, this healing came from welcoming the silence, from learning to communicate in different forms, from realizing that my "voice" transcended the sound I was able to create. All of these small acts shared something. None of them were an attempt to wipe out loss or give us back what we knew before they created new patterns. They accept absence as a fact. But they also create new traditions and habits and ways of living. They are what makes up the care for a wound, stitching one stitch after another into something that somehow holds together and eventually strengthens.

> *"Grief, I've learned, is just love. It's all the love you want to give but cannot. All of that unspent love gathers up in the corners of your eyes, the lump in your throat, and in that hollow part of your chest. Grief is just love with no place to go."*
>
> —Jamie Anderson

There Is No Greater Transformer Than Love

All four stories have the feeling that love does not end when you lose something or someone. This is probably the most redemptive thread through these experiences. Emma's love for her children didn't die with them. Instead, it widened its outward wings to include the shelter, to welcome some of the most vulnerable children. Every child she came in contact with now would be given some of the maternal love that had remained inside her heart. Both pain and purpose were turned into an inheritance from her children.

James's love for himself had felt like it dwindled, having been deeply connected to his work. When he lost that job, his identity and his sense of his place in the world felt futile. But he found that love with his brothers. Sharing his story was more about "feeding the sheep" the way God instructed rather than being starved by an experience that could have broken him.

Growing men in the word and truly helping them love themselves so they could love others was his way of holding onto faith.

Maya found her father's love lived on outside his very presence. It lived in his journals, in those lessons he'd taught her, and the way she spoke about advocacy.

Loss may have finished one page of their world story, but not all was ruined by it. I discovered that my voice—my actual voice—was never about just sound, tone, or diction. This was how I showed love, established relationships, and lived authentically. Even in silence, that voice remained. This thread instructs us that love and grief are not opposites but companions. From my life spent visiting grieving families, I have found that love follows grief from depth to depth.

Emma is grieving so deeply, because she's loved so deeply. James's silence is a testament to more than twenty years of dedication. Maya's anger and guilt reflect a father-daughter relationship that informed her entire worldview. And my tortured desire for my voice showed how crucial communication and connection are in my love.

It Takes a Village

None of these stories of healing emerged in isolation. We often use the teaching, "It takes a village to raise a child" when children are born, but its depth lasts a lifetime. Each person was in need of community, even if reluctantly so, to find their way forward.

Emma first alienated friends and family members, but, in time, found healing in group therapy and, eventually, in the children's shelter community. Suddenly, though, being vulnerable with other people to tell this story and to say out loud for the first time that her children were gone became a turning point.

James would resist any thought or inclination that he was depressed. It was easier for him to think of this time as doing the best he could as opposed to being open about his brokenness and his pain. He found solace in the place he least expected it, in his men's ministry brothers. Men that didn't characterize him as jobless but helped him to find the truth that he was still capable.

Maya's aunt even attempted to assist her in reviewing her father's things, to be with her as she went through them. But Maya healed later by being present for other people and seeing that supporting someone else didn't mean that she had grown past her own grief.

And I, even if I didn't speak, was kept warm by the community around me. The people who lived my painful life with words as no words could express, who walked with me through that valley. This thread uncovers a deeper truth that grief may be personal, but healing is communal. We need witnesses to our suffering, company who can relate, and in time, the chance of providing what was shared with us for others. The support group, the therapy session, the aunt's gentle handholding, the shelter's community, those are the places where isolated grief becomes shared resilience.

Living With, Not Moving Past: You Will Breathe Again.

Step back and read these stories side by side and you will realize there is a pattern across them, not a linear story but an endless dance between loss and re-creation. Through the lens of my own experience, I was able to see the dance happen through these stories.

- **There's the shattering:** The instant that our loss bursts into existence and upends the life we have known.
- **The unraveling:** Where the promised tomorrow vanishes and the spiraling begins.
- **The paralysis**: The necessary stillness, in which we can sit with how great things have been lost. This is not stagnation but gestation, during which grief performs work deep down below the surface.
- **The new beginnings:** The tentative, sometimes terrifying steps toward a new way of being. Not big acts of recovery, but the little steps: a letter written, a meeting attended, a diary opened, a silence admitted.

- **Transformation of love**: The finding that what we loved has not lost its way but has morphed into something new. Love becomes purpose, memory becomes direction, connection becomes legacy.
- **The expansion**: The point at which we realize that in fact, it is in offering something to others that, in a way, we are healing them, and we begin to realize it might be just as healing to us.

I believe Emma stands in the place of vulnerable children. James contributes his truth to other men of faith. Maya advocates for others. Using my restored faith and hope, I walk alongside others in their grief valleys. The most central thread among all these stories is this: None of these people "moved on" from their grief. This wisdom that runs through these experiences is called resilience. It is not going back to who we were prior to the loss. It is learning to inhabit the after, to shape our life around an absence, to form new rituals, to find a new sense of meaning, and to carry our loved ones in ways that are renewed.

The idea of moving past conveys the sense of leaving behind the person or the experience as though it is no longer necessary. These narratives teach us that healing isn't abandonment so much as integration. Emma still grieves for her children. "Grief is still with me," she says, "but it's something that we all share in love now." James knows that "grief doesn't leave you," but he found a joy of a different kind. Maya discovered that healing "didn't mean forgetting or 'overcoming' the loss," but "learning to hold onto my love for my father in new ways." And I hold onto the memory of my ten days in silence as "not a wound, but a reminder of the strength that comes by surrendering to a process of healing."

CHAPTER 7

FINDING HOPE BEYOND GRIEF

What I discovered in the quietest moments shaped the way I would later grapple with the more profound sorrows of those in life. I learned that what made us human is what connected us all. That our identity is fragile, that connection is sacred, and that moving forward demands that we submit to the process rather than struggle against it. I accepted that my parents and my brothers were gone, but my sense of their presence was forever changed. My voice returned, but I was forever changed by that experience as well. I had reached my breaking point with not doing anything, and in this, I learned that resilience is not found in bouncing back the same. It's making new things through those experiences of not being. It was pointless to stress over what I failed to get back. The benefit is found in learning to focus on how this has made me a better, different person.

As we study Emma's, James's, and Maya's journey compared to my own, four very strong threads pull their and my experiences together. First, grief is not just an end. It can also be a beginning. Second, through the pain, we are given the chance to grow in ways we might never have imagined. Third, in this time, we are forced to examine what matters most, to redefine who we are, and to carry forward the legacy of what we've lost. Fourth, finding hope beyond grief does not mean leaving it behind—it means learning to live with it, to let it shape us without letting it destroy us.

Finding hope is to first understand how you have been changed, what you want to do with that change, and what to hold onto as you navigate the new world of change. I learned and experienced that grief doesn't just take something from us. It fundamentally alters who we are. The person who existed before the loss cannot be fully recovered, and the sooner we stop trying to return to that former self, the sooner we can begin the real work of healing. Hope doesn't emerge from denying this transformation, but from acknowledging it with courage and curiosity.

The first step toward hope requires honest inventory. Grief remakes our foundation. Our priorities become different, our vulnerabilities more visible, our empathy more profound, our tolerance for superficiality reduced. We may be more wary and, ironically enough, more willing to take chances because we've already survived the unthinkable. Some changes are unwelcome—the anxiety that wasn't there before, the way joy now comes tinged with guilt, the heightened vigilance regarding loss. Yet other changes carry unexpected gifts. The profound appreciation for ordinary moments, deeper connections with those who stayed, clarity on what truly matters. To find and trust hope, we must see ourselves clearly in our new form. The new visibility is not aimed to see one as better or worse than before, but undeniably different. This acknowledgment isn't surrender but recognition. We cannot build a future on the foundation of who we used to be. We must build on who we have become.

Finding hope after grief does not follow the same path as one seeking optimism to get through a tough situation. It's not the naive belief that everything will be okay, or that time heals all wounds, or that we "get over it." Hope is much quieter, more resilient than that. Hope lies in getting out of bed, despite the fact that the weight of grief makes those blankets feel like concrete. Hope is when you can laugh without immediately drowning in guilt. Hope is planting a garden you may not feel like tending, trusting that future-you might want flowers. Hope is telling your story one more time, to one more person, because connection matters more than comfort. Hope is the decision that we make daily, sometimes hourly, accepting that while we cannot control what happens to us, we retain sovereignty over how we carry it forward.

"My hope is built on nothing less than Jesus' blood and righteousness; I dare not trust the sweetest frame, but wholly lean on Jesus' name."

—Edward Mote

Hope: The Golden Thread Throughout the Stages

For some, hope emerges as a distinct stage or thread that weaves through the entire grieving process. Hope is what reminds us that the darkness will not last forever, that we can find meaning even in the face of profound loss. Hope was the rope that kept me from falling. It might appear as a small glimmer in the most unexpected times and places through the process, but believe in it, cling to it, have faith in it. Whether it's a moment of laughter, a memory that brings warmth instead of tears, or the realization that life still holds beauty.

Even in the earliest stages of grief, when denial feels like our only protection against unbearable reality, hope is present. It is often disguised as resistance to loss itself, but it is still a form of hope that has to morph as you adapt to changing realities. The initial "no" that rises up in response to devastating news contains within it the seed of hope. The conviction that what we have lost matters enough to fight for, that the world should not be a place where such losses occur, that love is worth the fierce protection we offer it even in its absence—that is hope.

During my weeks of voice loss, my initial denial took the form of expecting each day to wake up with my voice restored. This daily disappointment was painful, but it also maintained my connection to the hope that healing was possible. Without this hope, even in its naive early form, I might have surrendered to despair and stopped doing the speech therapy exercises that eventually contributed to my recovery. The hope embedded in denial is often immature and unrealistic, but it serves the crucial function of keeping us engaged with life until we can develop more sophisticated forms of hope.

This early hope requires gentle tending rather than harsh correction. When someone in fresh grief speaks of their loved one in present tense or makes plans as if nothing has changed, they are not demonstrating pathology but preserving the hope necessary for eventual healing. The task of loving companions is not to force reality upon them but to hold space for both their denial and the hope it protects, trusting that time and love will gradually allow for more complex understandings to emerge.

This practice of navigating through the stages of grief and holding onto hope through it all takes courage. The cyclical nature of these stages means accepting that hope can come without proof, that we can and must work for a future, even when all evidence tells us it is impossible, that we can still live our lives tethered to other people and other ideas because true meaning doesn't need the guarantee of permanence. It is the courage of the gardener who plants in the spring, though she knows that winter will come again, the courage that trusts in growth even when the end is inevitable.

The journey does not call for perfect optimism but matured hope. Hope that has been tested by loss and turned out to be as strong as despair. This is not hope that one finds easily, hence why I say matured, as opposed to found. A person who has lost a sibling might find hope in supporting others who have experienced similar losses. Someone grieving the end of a relationship might discover hope in the possibility of new connections. It is not that the hope believes bad things won't happen but that we will find ways to make good things even after bad things. It is the hope, not that we can get back to who we were before we lost, but that we can become someone new. Someone with new passions, new desires, with a possession of loss, but not possessed by it.

For those of us on the grief path, navigating through is not an invitation to fast-forward through these stages but an opportunity to not judge ourselves for not "getting" to it fast enough. Grief cannot be hurried or fabricated. It can only be given as a process that arrives in its own time and evolves with time. Let this be the tender dawning that comes after a dark night of suffering. Rather than turning back time to a day that once was, usher in something entirely new, something that remembers the shadows we've traveled through even as it takes hold of the light that still streams into the world. Here in that dawn, we find ourselves to be both exposed and mending, mourning and giving thanks, forever scarred by loss and forever able to love. This is the miracle of grief, not that it removes our sadness, but that it instructs us how to mourn in hope.

Hope doesn't erase grief, but it transforms it. Hope is a reminder that while grief changes us, it does not define us. The golden thread of hope that weaves through our grief never breaks, though it may sometimes become so fine as to be nearly invisible. In our darkest moments, it may seem absent entirely, but patient attention reveals its presence in the smallest acts of continuation. The decision to eat when we have no appetite, the choice to answer the phone when we want only silence, the willingness to let others help when we prefer isolation.

For those walking the difficult path of grief, the invitation is not to manufacture hope but to remain open to its presence in whatever form it takes. Hope may appear as anger that refuses to surrender to helplessness, as bargaining that maintains faith in possibility, as depression that preserves the capacity for deep feeling, or as acceptance that believes in meaningful life beyond loss. In every stage, hope is present, weaving the golden thread that ultimately leads, not away from grief but through it, not around love but deeper into it, not toward forgetting but toward a remembering that transforms both memory and future into sources of sacred meaning.

This is the gift of hope-carried grief. It teaches us that love is stronger than death, that meaning can emerge from meaninglessness, and that we are capable of bearing far more than we ever imagined. Not because we are strong in ourselves, but because we are held by a hope that is larger than our circumstances, deeper than our pain, and more enduring than any loss we will ever face. In learning to grieve hopefully, we discover not just how to survive loss but how to let loss transform us into more loving, more compassionate, more deeply human beings. And perhaps that transformation is hope's greatest gift of all.

It is important to remember that no two people grieve in the same way. The stages Kübler-Ross described are not in an order set in stone without revision, but a guide to help us understand the emotional terrain of loss. I like to think of them as floors, and we are on the elevator navigating through them. Some people may never feel anger, while others might skip straight to depression or acceptance. Others might revisit a stage months or years later, triggered by a memory or milestone. What matters is not how we navigate the stages, but that we allow ourselves the space to grieve. There is no "right" way to process loss, no timeline to follow. Each stage serves a purpose, helping us confront our emotions and move toward healing in our own time and our own way.

In the end, the stages of grief are not a destination. They are a compass, pointing us toward healing. They remind us that it's okay to feel lost, angry, or heartbroken, and that these emotions are part of what makes us human. By honoring each stage, we honor our own journey and the love that lies at the heart of our grief. And through that love, we find the strength to carry on.

The Altered Self

Emotionally

Emotions are things we learn from our childhood stages. We learn what it means to be angry or sad as we lose toys or lose arguments with our siblings. And as we mature we give these emotions new depths as we encounter new instances that challenge the way we think about emotions, expressing these emotions, and living with them. Grief makes us face the rawest nature of our emotions because it leaves us feeling forever changed.

I had felt pain, sadness, hurt, fatigue, anxiety, and uncertainty all before, but my past experiences were nothing compared to what I felt as I navigated the initial instances of loss. At first, these emotions can be like a storm that will never pass. They rattled me and made me feel discomfort in times and places that were unplanned and nuanced. It moved the meter for the depth at which my body and mind were able to feel these matters and thus adjusted the lens by which I saw everything around me. I now saw everything through the trauma lens of loss.

This altered lens fractured my emotional understanding and awareness of life around me. Feelings that were once straightforward became complicated. For the first time, joy felt guilty, anger felt scary, numbness felt like failure. There were times where I felt immense amounts of emotion, and times where I felt nothing at all, even though I "should" have. The landscape and understanding I had of my emotional intelligence had become undone, but it was undone with reason. I began to accept that reason over time and invite hope in as my anchor. I soon realized that feeling deeply is not weakness, but rather, it was my emotional capacity widening to provide me the tools to emotionally adapt in this new season.

When my mother passed in 2015, my father in 2016, and my brothers following in 2017, 2018, and 2024, the rage was all-consuming. I was drowning in anger and overwhelmed by the unfairness. The anger had no clear direction. It was at God, at myself for all the conversations I'd never get to have, at family and friends for not doing enough. For months, I tried to push those feelings away, thinking anger had no place in grief. But slowly, I realized that my rage was love with nowhere to go.

Learning to dwell with emotion, especially those not connected to enjoyment, and allowing them to exist without judgment, opened my heart in unexpected ways. My emotional change was not rooted in the fact that I should no longer feel. Rather, it was rooted in the hope and knowledge that God contained all the grace to allow me to be angry, emotional, and hurt with Him, yet still not reject me or take His hand away from me.

The person I grew into through this period of repeated loss developed me into a more authentic state than I had ever been in before. I learned that I had grown to be a better, more emotionally aware person. Someone emotionally aware enough to hold space and empathy for the depths of my feelings but also for people I would encounter that feel as though no one else understands. This emotional depth can make us more compassionate, not just toward others, but toward ourselves. We learn that tears are not signs of breaking but of breaking open. We discover that our hearts, once cracked by loss, let in more light than we ever thought possible. The person you become through grief is not damaged goods but someone who has loved so deeply that loss could reshape you entirely. That's not something to fix. It's something to honor.

Physically

The truth is, the body remembers what the mind tries to forget. Throughout this book I have accounted for the instances of physical processing that grief pushed me to explore, willingly or unwillingly. When thinking of loss, it's easy to fathom that it is something that would be confined to one's heart. But I can admit, your heart is only the first stop loss makes on its points of choice along the way. It can feel like a weight on our chest, a knot in our stomach, or an ache in our bones. Sleep might elude us, or we might find ourselves sleeping too much. Energy levels plummet, and the simplest tasks can feel insurmountable.

The research tells us that grief triggers changes in our endocrine, immune, autonomic nervous, and cardiovascular systems. These are points I learned throughout and very early on in my studies of psychology. These are all fundamentally influenced by how our brain processes loss. But knowing the science didn't make it easier for me to get out of bed. I had no time to understand how or why cortisol and adrenaline were cascading through my system or that my immune function had dropped significantly. What I did understand was ache. I understood stuck, I understood empty, and I understood bodily rejection.

But here is what I've learned about the body and hope: Just as grief can rewire the brain toward suffering, healing can rewire it toward wholeness. Just as grief changes our bodies, it also teaches us to care for them. Over time, we learn to listen to what we need, whether it's rest, movement, nourishment, or simply a moment to breathe. Grief reminds us that our bodies carry our pain, and in caring for them, we honor that journey. My heart, that organ that once raced with panic, that pumped stress hormones through my bloodstream like poison, learned to beat with purpose, not just pain. Not forgetting, never forgetting, but keeping it differently. Holding my parents and my brothers not as an absence but as legacy. Carrying their love forward as a mission. The physical changes grief brings aren't obstacles to overcome. They're part of the sacred work of integrating loss into our lives. Your tired body is a body that has loved deeply. Your aching heart is a heart that has been stretched by loss and love. These changes deserve tenderness, not judgment.

This is what hope looks like after loss. It's not the absence of grief, but the presence of God within it. It is the anchorage to hold onto Him in some way, even when it may not be immediately clear. It's not the denial of pain, but the belief that pain can be redemptive. Not the restoration of what was, but the creation of what can be. My faith didn't protect me from grief's navigation through my body. But it gave me somewhere to bring that broken body, that broken vessel, and gain physical mending.

Relationally

Relationships go through some of the most intense shifts as one engages with the landscape of grief. I saw relationships that were "solid," in my opinion, crumple to their last strings of faith while I navigated loss and repair. It was hard for me. As someone who is intentional about who I connect with personally and deeply, there were times I imposed my expectation for more on them. Whether that be more conversation, more check-ins, more activity, I just wanted more. One of the most unsettling aspects of grief is the sudden sense of isolation it can create. You might find yourself surrounded by people yet feeling profoundly alone. I even held it against them at times.

How could they not see that I was in a constant ache? How could they not see that I was broken? Why did they not show up for me the way I had showed up for them when they experienced loss? And as I navigated the stages, I realized that the root of these questions was anger. It became easier to take my frustration out on those closest to me, to make them guilty of crimes they had not committed, in an effort to find someplace fitting for the pain I felt inside.

Grief unintentionally sorts our relationships. This sorting can feel like a secondary loss, compounding our pain, and shifting our mind to impose reasoning that is often incorrect. The danger of this lies not in the fact that you have created reason to justify the sorting, but that subconsciously, you begin to act on your interpretation. For example, when your partner's grief looks different from yours, it's easy to interpret their response as not caring enough, or not loving the person you lost as deeply as you did, or moving on too quickly. Therefore, you attack their processing. You become cold and distant because you feel that you are doing what feels justified, as they are not respectful of your pain. These interpretations, however understandable, can create a chasm that grows wider with each misunderstood moment, straining a relationship that is in need of hope and love.

Grief can reveal the strength of certain bonds while challenging us to let go of relationships that no longer serve us. Understanding these relational changes is not about judging them as good or bad, but about recognizing them as a natural part of the grieving process and an invitation toward hope. As I am connected to so many, it never crossed my mind that there would come a time where I felt alone, abandoned, and isolated. People I thought would be pillars of support disappeared, and I was unable to face the rawness of loss or the depth of what it felt like to feel distanced. And as I evolved and learned to live with, as opposed to move beyond, what I found the most beneficial to apply to my rawness was grace.

Grace for those who were unable and grace to accept those who were able. For those who step away not from lack of care but from their own fear and discomfort with mortality and suffering. These ones were often lacking the emotional capacity to witness my pain, as they may have been confronting their own unprocessed grief that my loss awakened. While their absence hurt, I prayed to be understanding, to allow compassion for them to heal me and better understand relational transition in grief. The relational changes grief brings are not detours from healing. They are opportunities I learned to hold onto as hope for a new tomorrow. As we learn to relate differently to others and to ourselves, we're not just surviving loss. We're being transformed by what it means to love and build community around us. And in that transformation, however painful, lies the possibility of more authentic, meaningful connection than we knew before.

Spiritually

My spiritual life has been forever altered by loss. I often think back to my darkest spiritual moments while navigating the initial shock and unraveling of grief and groan in pain. This was a time my mind was flooded with questions. These questions were never signs of weakness or failure. They were evidence that I am human. When we experience these moments, it's because we love deeply, and we're brave enough to sit with uncertainty. When we lose someone we love, the ground beneath our spiritual feet shifts. The beliefs that once felt solid, can suddenly seem fragile, or the actions that brought comfort and connection to God feel hollow and disconnected.

Within the weeks that followed losing my parents, I prayed but didn't feel connected to my prayers. The feelings of emptiness were not gone after losing my mother, and only worsened after losing my father a year and a half later. I lamented to Him, as it felt like the most fitting place to bring in my pain, and it helped me to still pray. Speaking to Him about anything else felt disconnected.

It was through a moment in worship the Lord revealed to me that I was checked out. Yes, I was there physically, but I was mentally absorbed by the pain of the flesh and immune to the potential restoration of the Father. My mind and heart had clung more to what I felt as a result of physical loss, as opposed to my faith in Him, and what it meant that my parents were no longer physically present. When the realization hit me, I could do nothing but beg God for forgiveness for coming into His presence in this manner. This disorientation is part of grief's transformation.

As the pain of loss captures all our senses, our body, and our being, it is to be expected that our spiritual life would encounter a shift, as all other parts of us do. But finding hope beyond grief is to again, first, do an honest inventory. I was pouring spiritually from an empty place. But because this space was unfamiliar, it became easier to follow routine spiritual acts. Although I found myself in His presence empty, it was in His presence that I found conviction and hope. It was in His presence I could find an explanation for the void I felt but could not name. In His presence, I felt the closest thing to the embrace of the ones I lost. I needed to be in His presence.

My altered self pushed me to pray differently, looking at laments as opportunities to invite God to wipe my tears. It was my invitation for Him to restore my peace. And it was also being respectful of the room He allows through grace and mercy for me to be upset and hurt. Within this spiritual upheaval, an evolved sense of hope emerged. Not the naive hope that everything will return to how it was, but a deeper, more resilient hope that learned to coexist with sorrow. It was there, at that intersection, that I felt one of the most meaningful connections to God. This hope doesn't erase the pain. Instead, it grows through it, the way roots push through rocky soil.

I understand more now what Edward Mote meant when he said, "When darkness veils his lovely face, I rest on his unchanging grace." Darkness, in this case loss, reared its head in my life for a season that felt like forever. Loss will shift your understanding of faith and will leave you with questions about the presence and love of God. But the questions grief brings can become doorways rather than dead ends. "Why did this happen?" might soften into "How do I carry this?" or "What matters most now?" These aren't easier questions, but they're ones that show alteration and ones that allow movement rather than paralysis. They are questions one must rest on His unchanging grace to answer.

Finding Growth Through Loss: Holding onto Hope

Allow New Perspectives on Grief and Loss

As we move through grief, our understanding of it evolves. What once felt like an unbearable weight becomes something we learn from and share, not something that defines and destroys us. This new perspective allows us to see grief not just as an end, but as a teacher. It shows us the depth of our love, the strength of our resilience, and the boundless capacity of the human spirit to heal. Grief has fundamentally changed how I see the world. It stripped away the trivial and revealed what truly matters. It provided a deeper sense of what it means to be alive. At one point that meant just breathing and going about my daily routines and expectations. But I understand now that this means navigating a world without heroes I thought would live forever. It means holding onto faith to learn to *live with* as opposed to *getting over*. And it also means continually encouraging myself to evolve spiritually, mentally, and emotionally instead of just waiting on traumatic life events to forcefully make this shift for me.

In my darkest moments, I discovered insights I never would have found in comfortability. Lessons about impermanence, connection, and the preciousness of each ordinary day. These perspectives didn't arrive all at once. They emerged gradually, like light breaking through clouds, after I gave myself permission to unravel. Now, I've learned that honoring these new understandings, honoring emotions, especially those not connected to peace, isn't just about getting through grief. It's about allowing loss to refine me for the better, leading to a better sense of self.

Five ways I've found and lived by these new perspectives:

1. **Be present: Practice intentional awareness in everyday moments.**

   Grief taught me that nothing is guaranteed, so I no longer save my attention for "special occasions." I've stopped waiting for life to happen and started recognizing that there is nothing like the present. The smaller the movement, the more remarkable the recognition.

2. **Understand that two things can be true.**

   For a while, I felt that happiness meant betraying my grief or being disrespectful to the memory of what I'd lost. Now I understand that this new version of self carries both. I am comforted by the fact that laughing doesn't invalidate my loss, and that honoring loss doesn't mean refusing comfort. I allow myself to experience all that it means to be human, without guilt or contradiction, because I know that my anchor is in Christ.

3. **Speak truth to what matters.**

   Grief burned away my tolerance for surface-level conversations and false representations of reality. I tell people I love them when hanging up the phone. I take pictures, not afraid to smile in the moments that matter. I ask for help when I need it. I share my truth even when it's uncomfortable. I speak out against injustice with love and correction, as I know I am a steward of God's people. This vulnerability has deepened my relationships and connections in ways I never expected. We are surrounded by fluff that is not helpful to our existence and hinders us living honest lives.

4. **Priorities are focused on meaning, not productivity.**

   I used to measure my days by what I accomplished, how busy I was, how much I checked off the list. I became addicted to being busy, so much so that when loss tore my world apart, the routine of overstimulation became my safety. Loss showed me how little those metrics of productivity actually matter. My gauge of what matters is different now than before. I ask, did I show up with love? Am I living and showing up in the way God would want me to? Did I make space for rest and reflection? These questions may be small, but they are impactful.

5. **Create moments to reflect that honor both memory and growth.**

   I've found ways to keep my loss present without letting it consume me. Singing my mother's favorite song, writing in my journal in silence to capture the gift that is solitude, cooking my father's favorite meal, visiting places my brother always wanted to go, and engaging in family time that honors their legacy. These moments aren't about staying stuck in the past. They are opportunities to integrate what I've lost into who I'm becoming. They remind me that grief and growth aren't opposites. Rather, they are companions on the same journey forward.

Embrace New Passions

Loss reshaped my routines and the terms I used to define myself. In order to "cope" at the time, I discovered passions, activities, and interests that brought purpose into the space. Some were things I had done before but never really committed to long term. Others were things I would have never explored if loss hadn't cracked me open and forced me to rebuild from the inside out. Nevertheless, they helped make my new normal functional. Clearing my mind at the gym in the mornings before the start of my day or enjoying a podcast devotion before bed—these allow for the glimpse of hope I needed to continue to rear its head.

When everything familiar was stripped away, I found myself asking questions I'd never made time for before: What actually brings me alive? What would I allow myself to do if I weren't afraid? What parts of myself have I been neglecting? The answers surprised me. I discovered that loss, confinement, and solitude had cleared space for refreshing new opportunities. Not as a replacement for what I'd lost, but as an expansion of who I was yet to become. Although new, I welcome the unknown, as they didn't feel frivolous or like distractions from my pain. Instead, they were life vests, like ways of honoring my own resilience and reclaiming my right to smile again.

Three ways I've found new passions and committed to them:

1. **Follow your curiosity without demanding it make sense.**

   I gave myself permission to explore things that intrigued me, even if they seemed random or impractical. I took a dance class on a whim. I started learning greetings in languages I'd always found beautiful. I didn't ask these interests to justify themselves or become something productive. I just let myself be a beginner again. It may seem futile, but it was an outward example of an internal need. I needed to see that there is hope in new beginnings again. This playful approach removed the pressure and allowed genuine passion to emerge naturally from what I considered a broken place, my heart.

2. **Create boundaries and accountability around what matters.**

   For something new to turn into a habit, you need dedicated time for it to resonate. Once I identified something that truly piqued my interest, I made it real by building it into my life intentionally. I blocked out time on my calendar, treating these commitments with the same respect I'd give to important appointments. I set small, achievable goals, not to prove anything, but to create momentum and a sense of progress. This structure transformed small opportunities into habits and routines, which started the work to rebuild my sense of belonging.

3. **Let passion and pain evolve on your journey.**

I've learned not to cling too tightly to any single interest or judge myself when what once brought joy no longer does. This allows me to understand and manage in the smallest of ways. Understanding that losing something, someone, isn't meant to break you. It's a means to groom you, and sometimes that's painful. Some passions were exactly what I needed for a season. They helped me process, distracted me when I needed distraction, or connected me to others when I felt isolated. Others have stayed and deepened over time. But for this cycle to happen, I had to give myself permission to release what no longer served me and remain open to what calls to me next.

Seek Acceptance of How Grief Enriches Our Lives

For a long time, I struggled with the idea that grief could be anything other than purely painful. But as I experienced different forms of loss and gained maturity in my understanding of the word, I have seen a multitude of ways that it is a teacher, enricher, and in some ways, a fulfiller. It felt like a betrayal to suggest that something so devastating could offer gifts. But as I've traveled deeper into this landscape, I've come to understand that acknowledging grief's transformative power doesn't diminish my loss. Instead, it honors the profound impact that gaining and losing love had on shaping who I am.

I've learned that grief doesn't just take from us. It also gives, sometimes in ways we don't recognize until much later. Accepting how grief enriches my life hasn't made it hurt less, but it has made the hurt mean something. Grief, painful as it is, makes us more present, teaching us to cherish the moments we have. It reminds us of the fragility of life, urging us to live with intention and gratitude. It carries the legacy in our actions, our choices, and the way we love others. Grief enriches our lives by showing us what truly matters and by shaping us into more compassionate, authentic versions of ourselves.

Four ways I've grown to accept and better understand how grief enriches my life:

1. **Learn to recognize grief as evidence, not just deep pain.**

   When the waves of sadness crash over me, I've started asking myself a different question: What does this pain tell me about how much I loved? Instead of rushing past the moment as a means of getting back to being okay, I acknowledge that every tear, every moment of longing, every ache of absence is actually a testament to a connection that mattered profoundly. This reimagining doesn't make grief easier, but it helped alter my relationship with what I knew of loss. Instead of seeing my grief as something to overcome or get past, I've come to understand it as the ongoing expression of a love that doesn't end just because someone is gone. With time, this has allowed me to hold my grieving experiences more gently, knowing that it is homage to something beautiful.

2. **Using familiarity as an opportunity to support, not fix.**

   There's a particular kind of recognition that happens now when I encounter someone else in pain. In the cries and groans, I often become emotional, as it speaks to a familiarity in my bones that I didn't have before loss. I can see the forced smiles, hear what's not being said, and feel the weight people carry invisibly. This has by no means made me an expert in grief struggles, but it has made me more aware and less judgmental. Instead of trying to offer the perfect words, I simply show up, sit with discomfort, and let people know they're seen. I now have an understanding that visibility is often holding space without needing to change or solve anything.

3. **Carrying someone's legacy forward gives grief purpose.**

   At first, remembering felt like torture. But gradually, I've found that honoring what mattered to the person I lost has become a way of keeping them present in my life. When I show kindness the way they did, or pursue something they encouraged in me, or make choices that would make them proud, I'm allowing their influence to continue shaping me. This has enriched my life by giving me a compass, a way of asking, "What would honor this person and their legacy?"

4. **Open yourself to the community that grief creates.**

   In my day-to-day life, I encounter a number of people. Whether on social media, in person, when traveling, or in the neighborhood, I am often surrounded by people. But as I redefined finding hope on this journey, I have found new layers in people that have suffered loss that have opened another layer of community I didn't know before—those who understand without explanation, who don't need me to be "better" yet, who can hold my sorrow without discomfort. Some are people I have known all my life, and others are new. I am thankful just the same. They've shown me that vulnerability creates intimacy, that shared pain can become shared strength, and that some of the most meaningful connections in my life came from the worst thing that ever happened to me.

The Role of Time

Time does not heal all wounds, but it does soften them. In the early days of grief, time feels like an enemy—stretching endlessly, amplifying the ache of loss. But as time passes, it becomes a gentle companion, helping us adjust to a new reality.

Time allows us to find balance. It doesn't erase what happened, but it helps us integrate our loss into the fabric of our lives. We learn to carry our grief alongside our joy, to hold sadness and gratitude in the same breath.

Finding Balance Without Forgetting

Once again, I want to stress that we don't "move on" from loss. We move forward with it. The memories of what we've lost remain a part of us, but they no longer weigh us down. Instead, they become a source of strength, a reminder of the love that shaped us and the resilience we've found.

Finding balance means giving ourselves permission to feel both the pain of what we've lost and the hope of what lies ahead. It means allowing ourselves to smile, to love, and to dream again, even as we carry the echoes of our grief.

Hope doesn't mean forgetting—it means believing that life can still hold beauty and meaning, even after loss. It means trusting that we have the strength to carry our grief while embracing the possibilities of the future. Grief changes us, but it also teaches us. Through its pain, we find growth, connection, and the courage to keep going. And in finding hope beyond grief, we honor not only what we've lost but also the enduring power of love to guide us forward.

CHAPTER 8

JOY AS CONFIRMATION OF HIS PROMISE

"Grief is not a disorder, a disease, or a sign of weakness. It is an emotional, spiritual, and physical necessity, the price you pay for love. The only cure for grief is to grieve."

—Earl Grollman

We have all heard the verse, "Weeping may endure for a night, but joy comes in the morning," but the part we often neglect is that to get to the joy, we have to live. We have to push on beyond the moment and press to progress. The ancient wisdom of these words never felt more hollow than as I sit and think of them now. I would wake in the darkness, that midnight hour darkness, and wonder if morning would ever truly come. In that moment, the night I'm speaking of wasn't measured in hours. It was a frame of time measured only in the weight of absence. My night lasted through the seasons. Through holidays that felt like vast terrains. Through the simple question of, "How are your parents?" asked by someone who didn't know. I desperately yearned for "morning." Not just the sunrise, but that morning. The one promised in the psalm. The one where joy was supposed to arrive like a guest I'd been waiting for. The one that would remove the gloom cast over me.

A very difficult part of learning to find hope again and living on is allowing ourselves to express joy again. After a loss, happiness can feel like a betrayal, a form of disrespect to the person or life they lived. It felt rude at times to smile, to laugh, to feel hopeful because the pain of grief loomed over me. I self-policed my feelings, not permitting myself to feel anything I told myself was unbefitting my pain. But the truth grief often blinds us to is that joy is not a betrayal. Joy is the product of resilience. Joy is the product of resisting the consuming nature of loss, standing firm that the joy of the Lord is your strength and rising above.

Feeling unguilted joy again takes time. Trapping ourselves in black-and-white thought processes prevents us from fully grieving or fully living. That is why I say that the stages of grief are to be seen as elevator floors, floors one will ride to for a lifetime to come. It's natural to exist in limbo, terrified that going forward means going backward in time to carefree joy. I have come to believe and show that joy does not wipe away grief—it adds to it. Imagine it as a colorful sweater, sewn by hand. Sadness and pain are the deep, rich braids to support the fabric and give it depth, while joy, laughter, hope, and compassion give the threads the vivid colors that render it beautiful. Grief without joy amounts to despair, and joy without the richness contained in having loved and lost misses the real appreciation that makes happiness so valuable.

Joy is a sign of life, and life is still worth living. It tells us we're more than our losses, that our ability to be happy didn't vanish before our eyes after we lost our dreams or our people. For many like me, who experience medical trauma or physical loss alongside bereavement, the injury to the body becomes aligned with the pain to identity and sense of self. My changed voice served as a constant, audible reminder of everything that had been taken from me, but I had to grow to see this as an event, not my life story. Granting ourselves permission to reclaim joy is not so much an opinion as it is an active choice. It's a conscious choice to stop apologizing for our mere existence. The permission comes at a moment where it feels unlike what is expected of us. We've gotten used to the heft of grief so much that lightness seems artificial, even wrong. You could catch yourself in a true laugh and then suddenly find yourself flooded with guilt for having "forgotten." But those moments of awakening uncover the potential for growth.

We do not have to close out the joy. There is no instruction in life that says one must be sad and broken forever to grieve. Finding my way back to joy taught me that sometimes it's required to lose control of something very basic and fundamental, something as simple as our voice, to fathom the depth of what living means. The period of silence forced me to find other ways to connect with life, other ways to honor my parents' memory, and other ways to sit in joyous moments around me. When joy finally returned, it came with a profound gratitude, not just for happiness itself, but for the capacity to express it, to share it, to let it resonate in the world through words and laughter and the simple miracle of being heard.

To describe the story of Job without mentioning this balance is simply to describe the events. It is not hidden that Job had lost everything, his children, his wealth, his health. There were moments where he sat in the ashes of his former life. His wife advised him to curse God and die, to acknowledge the inevitability of his suffering. But Job's story does not give in to the ashes. God restores Job's fortunes, his faith, and his victory after his profound grief and spiritual wrestling. What makes Job's story so remarkable is not only that he was blessed again, but it's that he was able to receive those blessings, that he opened his heart when he had every reason to remain dark and closed. He didn't reject his new children because they weren't his old children. He did not reject prosperity as a betrayal of losses. Job grasped the openness that is the renewal and the rising from the ashes. As he welcomed new joy, it did not take the love that he had for what was lost away. And his ability to accept being alive after his loss, with all of the sorrow that he carried, tells us that mended memories don't have to be abandoned in the service of healing.

Finding joy may start small, and that's just the way it should be done. Walking in the sun when you see the warmth on your face for the first time in ages and months. A song people remember to hum in your ear before they realize they're supposed to be sad. A moment of real, genuine, organic laughter that suddenly rises up between two friends is one that is free from some of the heavy air it usually takes to be in touch with them. These are not minor slips in the life course, little betrayals, but invitations to be revived. The prophet Nehemiah had this in mind when he commanded the Israelites, "Do not grieve, for the joy of the Lord is your strength." This wasn't a negation of their very real sorrows or struggle, as they were in a real moment of pain. They had recently heard about the destruction of Jerusalem and cried out loud, but Nehemiah had lived this moment before. That allowed him to voice with confidence that joy is not just a feeling. It is an act of strength. It's what allows us to carry on, recover, and move ahead. The Israelites' joy was not out of proportion to their circumstances, and it was vital for their survival and recovery.

The morning that comes is in no way saying there is an absence of night. It's the presence of light strong enough to exist alongside the darkness. It's learning that you can carry sorrow in one hand and joy in the other, that you can lose pieces of yourself and still be whole. Growth after one's trauma doesn't mean the trauma was good or that we're glad it happened. As Tedeschi and Calhoun emphasize, growth and distress coexist. Positive changes don't erase the negative impact of loss.[20] Rather, growth emerges from the struggle with trauma's aftermath, from the cognitive processing required to rebuild a shattered worldview. It's not about bouncing back to baseline but about transformation beyond previous levels of functioning. Weeping may endure for the night, and the truth is, sometimes the night is long. But remember, you have seen daylight before, and it feels amazing. Joy does come in the morning. Not because grief ends, but because you learn to live anyway. You learn to sing with a different voice. You learn to love what remains. You learn to build pillars strong enough to support a life that includes loss and still reaches toward the light.

The Courage to Choose Life. Feeling Joyous Again

Choosing joy after loss takes considerable bravery. Every aspect of our lives is involved when joy disappears after a loss. The absence of joy isn't just

20 Tedeschi, R. G., & L. G. Calhoun. (1996). "The Posttraumatic Growth Inventory: Measuring the positive legacy of trauma." *Journal of Traumatic Stress, 9*(3), 455-471.

about feeling sad. It is losing our sense of aliveness, our connection to meaning, and our ability to envision a future worth living. Grief without joy becomes a suffocating weight that colors everything gray. We go through the motions of daily life, but nothing feels vibrant or worthwhile. Food loses its taste. Laughter feels foreign and uncomfortable. Activities that once brought pleasure no longer make sense or draw us in, leaving us empty and deserted. Perhaps most profound of all, without joy, we no longer yearn for hope. Hope and joy are deeply connected. Joy gives us the feeling that good things are still possible, that beauty still exists, that we are still capable of experiencing the fullness of life—that is hope. The loss of joy, then, is not simply the absence of joy. It's about losing our connection to the belief that life can be meaningful and good again, even after devastating loss.

It means putting your life on the line with no confidence. This process must come to terms with acceptance that life will never be the same. It means honoring our grief but not letting that grief completely determine us. One may ask, Well, how do I get there, and how do I maintain this sense of joy once I have acquired it? The important thing to note is that you should not fear failed attempts. I remember there were times I was truly trying to be happy and joyful doing something to honor my pain, and instead, it made me sadder. Sometimes the result is sadness, and that's all right. Some days it's anger, or fear, or confusion, and that's fine too. But other times, perhaps more often than we expect, actual happiness, peace, or delight is what occurs. When these moments arrive, our job is not to analyze, question, or feel guilty about them. It's to thank God for them and live in the moment.

The challenge we face is to receive them as gifts. They remind us that we're still alive, still capable of experiencing the full spectrum of human emotion, still deserving of joy. Joy comes back, not because we have forgotten how we have hurt, but because we have chosen to let light penetrate the darkness. Scripture tells us that "the joy of the Lord is your strength" and that we can "count it all joy," even in trials. Joy is an act of rebellion against the despair that will swallow us up. That is a testimony to the fact that darkness doesn't get the final word. Joy isn't an atonement for our losses. We respect our losses by not allowing mourning to overshadow the goodness that still exists, by saying that life and hope endure even in the midst of loss.

That does not mean trying to stifle happiness or faking it when we're not normal. Real joy can't be put together, but it arises when we open space, when we stop pushing away from it, when we give ourselves permission to feel the way things actually feel. Our task is to accept it all as gifts, let the process be a reminder that we're still alive, capable of holding onto the spectrum of emotional experience full of possibilities. Joy comes back, not as though we have long forgotten the hurt that we so deeply feel, but because we've learned to carry it differently. With joy we don't devalorize our losses. We acknowledge them and refuse to let them steal any of the fullness of our lives that we still have from them.

Ways to Feel Joyous Again

Gratitude as a Source of Joy

Gratitude stems from the tree of joy. It is a product of one being open to the possibility of living a new version of life. In the midst of my darkest days, when everything felt heavy and dark, the simple act of noticing what remains became a lifeline. The simple act of thinking of all the ways we are blessed and have been blessed began to give me glimpses of joy again in my spirit. I began to thank God profusely for the small things, the big things, the past things—unknown things. This moment unknowingly brought back to my face and my soul something I had not known in some time, a genuine smile, a genuine sense of joy.

Gratitude doesn't deny the reality of our pain or make efforts to state that everything is fine. Instead, it considers that although we may endure our darkest valleys, there are still glimmers of light worth recognizing. When we choose to be grateful for all the love we have around us, for the people who are still with us, and for the breath in our bodies, we are making a declaration. We are saying, "Yes, I may walk through the valley of the shadow of death, but THOU art with me." We are saying that loss, though devastating, has not stripped us of everything. Gratitude shifts our gaze from what has been taken to what remains, from what we cannot control to what we can still receive.

The Apostle Paul explicitly states this connection as he writes, "Rejoice evermore. Pray without ceasing. In every thing give thanks: for this is the will of God in Christ Jesus concerning you." (1 Thessalonians 5:16-18) See the progression: rejoicing and thanksgiving are part of the same stance (faithfulness), like the same garment. Paul is not proposing we refuse to acknowledge our pain, pretending that it is not present. Instead, he's showing that gratitude is a tool for moving from that which you don't have to the things that you can, and it provides room for joy. And yet Paul writes from prison in Philippians, a place of literal darkness and loss, but proclaims that you should, "Rejoice in the Lord always: and again I say, Rejoice.!" (Philippians 4:4) A few verses later, he says, "Be careful for nothing; but in every thing by prayer and supplication with thanksgiving let your requests be made known unto God. And the peace of God, which passeth all understanding, shall keep your hearts and minds through Christ Jesus."(Philippians 4:6-7) Here, thanksgiving is the way to peace and joy that transcends situations. And when we bring our needs to God with grateful hearts, acknowledging His faithfulness even as we are suffering, we are able to experience a joy we cannot achieve ourselves or gain through nothing.

This transformation took time for me, and it will take time for all those that will visit this valley at some point in their lives. This gratitude, like hope, never aims to erase the reality that one feels with loss, but it allows us something fulfilling to replace the void. Over time, as you practice noticing the good and being thankful for it, gratitude becomes a spring of joy. It reminds us that you are still alive, that you are still capable of believing, and still surrounded by grace. And with that recognition, joy begins to take root again, not as a betrayal of our loss, but as a testament to our resilience.

Four Ways to Remember Gratitude as the Source of Joy

1. **Keep a daily gratitude practice.**

   In my journey of being intentional with time, I found gratitude to be something I didn't make enough time to acknowledge. To be better, I set aside time each day, even just a few minutes, to write down or reflect on three things I am grateful for. Some days they are profound, and others they are basic, but each day,

I carve out space for thankfulness. Over time, this practice trains your mind to notice goodness even among sorrow.

2. **Hide the joyous word in your heart.**

   The instances to grab joy often felt futile, especially on the days that were hard. Having the word in my heart, I used those verses to talk myself out of dark times, when I had no great sermon to preach to myself. That's what got me through. Hold onto the speaking of joy from the Bible. Speak it over yourself as your first words to God in the morning and your last at night. When gratitude becomes the beginning and end of each day, it gradually transforms how you see everything in between.

3. **Express gratitude to others.**

   It's one thing to make time for gratitude, but nothing if you are not sharing these instances of thanks with those around us. I no longer hesitate to tell people what they mean to me, and neither should you. When you overthink the value of these kind words, you miss opportunities to share the warm embrace that is love and joy. Make that phone call, send a text, or make that post. Share your appreciation for people's presence in your life, because it matters. When we acknowledge the ways others have blessed our lives, we create connections and remind ourselves that we are not alone.

4. **Reframe painful memories through a lens of thankfulness.**

   As I navigated the stages, there were many times I took a step back and instead of focusing on the loss I experienced, I found what there was to be thankful for in that moment. I have always been thankful for my parents, my brothers, and the role they played in my life. But it did take some time for me to state that while aching about their loss. Language matters. And, it is only through that adjustment to gratitude that joy will rear its head.

CHAPTER 9

PRACTICAL SUGGESTIONS FOR DEALING WITH GRIEF

Grief is not a passive experience. It requires us to be active participants in our healing, and for that, we must show ourselves acts of kindness first. While grief may come uninvited, our response to it can shape the path forward. And the tool you use to do the shaping is love. The apostle John said, "We love him, because he first loved us." (1 John 4:19) For years, I imagined I knew and used this verse in all the ways one could. I had thought it was only about gratitude, about reciprocity, about passing along what was given to me. But sitting in the wreckage of loss, I finally made sense of its larger landscape.

My losses left behind a frantic energy, a constant pressure to show that regardless of everything that had been taken away from me, I was still worthy of my space. By fixing everything else, it would make me have more validation. If I could not speak the way I did, I would write more. If I weren't able to save my parents or my brothers, I would save everybody else. I'd fix every broken thing I saw. I'd fight my way back to worthiness through exhaustion, no matter what it took. This is grief's most delicious lie. Telling our mind and body that we can outmaneuver our pain by needing to be indispensable to others. Fighting for the notion that if you simply help enough people and love enough people, and fix enough people, you won't have to live with the fact that you are shattered.

Before you can love outside, you take love inside. It is through God loving us first, that you felt loved, you took that love in, and that is what permits us to exude it to others. This would also mean that before you can give restoration to others, you need to let yourself be restored. Perhaps this is the most missed truth about grief. I learned that the truth about the way forward is not in fixing everything around us, or even fixing others to get better. It's in permitting and showing love and compassion. This looks like allowing yourself to not be okay. Allowing yourself vulnerability, allowing yourself community, and allowing yourself grace. Societal expectation has said that this is selfish. That love in its selfless nature looks outward before inward. But Jesus himself withdrew to solitary places to pray. (Luke 5:16) Even the Son of God recognized pouring out would require filling first.

In my second year after my brother's death, I began a practice that seemed unbearably vulnerable. I wrote a love letter to myself. Not affirmations or motivational speeches, but real-life letters showing compassion for me. Verbalizing what I loved about what it meant to be Clive. Not the pastor, the son, the father, the brother, the friend, but what it meant to be Me. I wrote about the resilience it requires to wake up every single morning. I wrote about the dimensions of my personality that are unique. And as the pen flowed across the paper, I could feel a new level of release come over me. I celebrated the small victories. Nothing grand, but a full day without crying, a moment of real laughter, the ability to think of them without my voice breaking.

At first it struck me as a bit self-centered. But it became apparent very gradually that this was just an act of living out the love God gave me. I was expressing myself, about myself, with empathy and grace. Not measuring why and how I did not meet the markers of processing I "should" have. As I became gentler with myself, I found that I had more gentleness in me to give to others. When I had better understood my own brokenness, without shame, I could be with others in their brokenness and not try to rush them to wholeness. I adjusted my framework, no longer pushing those who were new to loss or still living with it to believe that their old self is worth fighting to attain. Because with that, you deprive yourself of getting to know and love the new and evolved things about you.

This is the love of stewardship. Facing the reality that you have a single life, one body, one heart, and that caring for these is not selfishness or escape but sacred. As Paul explains, our bodies are temples of the Holy Spirit. (1 Corinthians 6:19) Engaging in self-care glorifies the temple and grounds its longevity.

- **Physical Self-Care** – You might feel exhausted, lose your appetite, or struggle to sleep. Paying attention to your physical needs is essential. Gentle movement, such as walking or yoga, can help release tension. Eating nourishing meals and staying hydrated provide the energy you need to cope. If sleep is elusive, try establishing a calming bedtime routine or seeking support from a healthcare provider.
- **Emotional Self-Care** – Find ways to nurture your spirit. Give yourself permission to rest, to cry, and to seek comfort in things that bring you peace—a favorite book, soothing music, or time spent in nature.
- **Spiritual Self-Care** – Stay spiritually aware of your surroundings, whether you find comfort in prayer, meditation, or simply spending time in quiet reflection, nurturing your spiritual well-being can provide a sense of grounding. For some, connecting with a faith community or exploring mindfulness practices may offer solace.

The foundational point is that grief has a way forward, not in exceeding our humanity but in embracing it. It is located in the knowledge our best selves cannot be at the service of others until you are there in some capacity of service with yourself. This is not a one-time instance, but a repetitive routine that one has to check themselves to ensure they are engaged with the truth.

On some days, it entails forcing yourself to take a shower, even when that could seem an impossible task when filtered through the eyes of depression. Other days, it may be choosing another form of self-care other than being with friends and going out, because you have to just exist without performing. At other times, it's seeking help. Because you are beloved. Not for what you did or how effectively you navigated your loss or how quickly you got back on your feet. Not because you have made something significant out of your trauma or fueled the fire of resilience for others. You are beloved precisely because you exist. Full stop. No qualifiers needed. When this is finally accepted, and you allow this truth to be the foundation of your broken places, it changes everything. There, you no longer punish yourself for not "healing" in another person's timeline. Only from that place of true self-love and attention can you first step forward.

The losses I have experienced echo in my mind without warning. The particular vibration of my mother's laugh that I can no longer perfectly recall, my father's handwriting on birthday cards I saved, my brother's way of seeing the world that died with him, the sound of my own voice before surgery reshaped it. These were not problems to be solved. They were realities to be integrated. And integration requires the kind of gentle, persistent love that we so rarely think to offer ourselves. It is a process, often messy and unpredictable, that asks us to engage with our emotions, our memories, and our pain.

Grief Requires Active Healing

As one heals from injury, so must you navigate processing grief. I don't consider it something that one is healed from. But in order to reuse the muscle or the body part after injury, one must heal the wounded parts of the body to process again. Healing from grief doesn't mean forgetting or "moving on." It means actively working to integrate our loss into our lives, learning to live with the pain while finding moments of peace and, eventually, hope. Active healing is described by Dr. Felkins as any technique that relies on patient participation to expedite healing. Active healing requires courage activation and full engagement to see and feel results.

Grief is not linear, and there is no right way to grieve. The thing that is often lost, that I learned and keep dear, is that healing is not about intensity. It's about consistency. In this healing journey, you are building a relationship, and it requires your attention, but also your patience. What works for one person may not work for another, hence I understand every approach may not fit all. But there is value in finding a structure for you to navigate this unknown territory. And with various approaches, the key is to be patient with yourself. Don't be afraid to try different approaches and to trust that healing, while slow, is possible. No matter the methods you navigate to actively heal, know that they are founded on these key principles:

1. Allow yourself to feel without judgment.
2. Name what you're experiencing.
3. Move your body intentionally.
4. Express your grief externally.
5. Practice self-compassion actively.

Story of Naomi

Naomi's story begins with loss. Loss of her connection to her home and people, and then to the family she had chosen. During a famine in Bethlehem, she moved to Moab with her husband, Elimelech, and their two sons. While living there her husband died, leaving her a widow in a foreign land. Her two sons married Moabite women, but then both sons also passed away within about ten years. Naomi found herself alone, grieving her life, her husband, and her children. She had lost not just her family but her entire future. Looking deeper, you see an added layer of loss—she lost her identity. As her identity was tied heavily to being a wife and mother, without her husband and children, she experienced a void that was both internal and external. When she heard that the famine in Bethlehem, her homeland, had ended, she decided to return. She urged her daughters-in-law to stay in Moab where they had better chances of remarrying, but she would be going home.

When Naomi returned to Bethlehem with Ruth (who insisted on coming), the whole town was stirred by her arrival. The women asked, "Can this be Naomi?" Her response reveals the depth of her grief: "And she said unto them, Call me not Naomi, call me Mara: for the Almighty hath dealt very bitterly with me. I went out full and the Lord hath brought me home again empty: why then call ye me Naomi, seeing the Lord hath testified against me, and the Almighty hath afflicted." (Ruth 1:20-21) Naomi was honest about her pain, her anger at God, and her sense of emptiness. Yet despite this raw grief, she continued to take steps forward. Her journey shows us that healing doesn't require pretending to be fine, but it requires honesty.

She Named Her Pain Honestly

Naomi didn't suppress or spiritualize her grief. When people greeted her, she honestly corrected them. Not with abuse or with harsh words, but her truth. She openly stated that God had afflicted her and brought her back empty. This naming of grief was important, her ability to say, "I am not okay." She wasn't in denial about her devastation. She gave voice to her anger, her loss, and her feeling of divine abandonment. Naomi modeled that faith doesn't require fake positivity. It can hold space for bitter truth-telling.

1. **She Kept Moving Forward Despite Immediate Circumstance**

   Although faced with devastation, Naomi continued to press forward, holding onto hope and her faith. She could have stayed shackled to the place that had been taken from her and decided to wither away, as she had already lost so much. But instead, she took action. Walking that hard journey home, facing the community who were sure to see just how much she'd lost, stepping back into a place where she'd have to rebuild everything. Movement matters in grief. Naomi teaches us that you don't have to feel hopeful about moving into the next phase or space, but you do have to move. She shifted her body, changed her location, and positioned herself for the possibility of healing to come to her, even though she did not presently see that possibility. That was hope.

2. **She Maintained Relationships and Accepted Support**

   Though Naomi told Ruth to leave her, she ultimately accepted Ruth's fierce commitment to stay. In grief, one will often feel that they are undeserving of good things, of community, of others' time and their compassion. Naomi accepted Ruth's commitment to stay did not come with strings nor expectation, but rather, fullness and love. This shows that active healing doesn't mean doing everything alone. Naomi let Ruth help carry the burden, and that relationship became a lifeline even when Naomi couldn't fully appreciate it yet.

3. **She Gradually Reengaged with Hope and Purpose**

   As the story progresses, Naomi begins to shift from passive healing to active processing and participation in life again. She notices Boaz and starts making plans for Ruth's security. She advises Ruth on how to approach Boaz and engages with the opportunity of their being together. In this moment of matchmaking, she subtly shows that she's thinking about the future again, not just dwelling in past loss. This wasn't instant healing. This was months after her loss that she gained the strength to think of love again. Slowly, Naomi moved from "I am empty" to "perhaps there's still possibility." She didn't force premature optimism. She let healing unfold and become her catalyst to more.

4. **She Allowed Joy to Return Without Guilt**

   By the end of the story, when Ruth and Boaz marry and have a son, the women of Bethlehem celebrate with Naomi: "Praise be to the Lord, who this day has not left you without a kinsman-redeemer. May he become famous throughout Israel! He will renew your life and sustain you in your old age." (Ruth 4:14-15) Naomi, who had returned "empty," now held her grandson. The text says, "Naomi took the child in her arms and cared for him." She didn't reject this new joy out of captivity to her grief. She didn't say, "I can't be happy because my sons are still dead." She held both realities simultaneously as her new identity. Her sons were gone *and* new life had come. This is the goal of active healing, the ability to experience joy again without betraying the memory of what was lost.

5. **The Transformation: From Mara to Naomi Again**

   The women of Bethlehem named Ruth's son Obed, but they said to Naomi, "And the women her neighbors gave it a name, saying, There is a son born to Naomi; and they called his name Obed: he is the father of Jesse, the father of David." (Ruth 4:17)

Her fullness was so radiant it could not be hidden. The community recognized her restoration as it shone bright through her. Naomi, who insisted she was Mara, bitter and empty, had become Naomi again through a process she couldn't have orchestrated herself. She didn't heal by denying her grief or by staying stuck. She healed by naming it honestly, continuing to put one foot in front of the other, accepting help, slowly reengaging with life's possibilities though home and faith, and ultimately allowing new joy to coexist with old pain. Her story teaches that active healing is both deeply personal work and something that happens in community, over time, through a mixture of our small faithful steps and grace we cannot manufacture ourselves, engagement with both pain and life.

"Moving on, as a concept, is for stupid people. Because any sensible person knows grief is a long-term project. I refuse to rush. Let no man slow, speed, or fix."
—Max Porter

Grief Requires Acceptance of Change

Grief changes us in ways we can't always predict. It strips away what is unimportant, forcing us to confront what truly matters. In the process, it transforms us. Throughout life, especially as you navigate active healing, you must remember the aim is to GROW. Grief is not just sadness. It is a complex mix of emotions that can include anger, guilt, confusion, and even moments of relief. Allowing these emotions to surface, rather than suppressing them, is vital for healing.

Grateful for Life's Special Moments

Grief sharpens our appreciation for life's fleeting beauty. You learn to cherish the people you love, to hold them close, and to savor the moments you have. After loss, it starts to dawn on us all in the small miracles you once ignored, the morning light, the laughter, the familiar things you hear around you. This new perspective is not about harmful positivity or making ourselves "look on the bright side." This is something rather real, digesting an acknowledgment that nothing lasts forever. Active healing through gratitude is the intentional choice to embrace the memory and the love shared with an open heart, creating the space to honor your loved ones by experiencing the world in all its complexity. The moment you acknowledge the love of the folks who are left to us with gratitude, you make strides to living in love the way God has called us. This practice is a bridge between sorrow and celebration, holding that much-needed pain, alongside all the gifts of presence in the world.

Resilient to Endure

Grief shows us how much you can endure. Some will say it's the worst pain they have ever felt, and to live beyond that is a testament to their strength. Others will say they are forever changed, and that also is another pillar of strength beyond immediate perception. The fact that you wake up each day, even when it feels impossible, is a testament to your strength. The resilience you find in grief is built from the times when you keep breathing despite feeling unimaginable pain. Healing with purpose is about recognizing that our healing must involve finding an anchor that grounds you as you work through this new normal.

The ability to get up from bed on the most difficult days is strength and hope combined. This strength does not come in the form of "moving on." This resilience may not always be internal. There may come times it has to be sought. Grief can feel overwhelming, and there is no shame in seeking help from a professional. Therapists, counselors, and grief specialists are trained to provide guidance and support as you navigate your loss. Don't wait until you feel desperate to seek help. Reaching out early can prevent your grief from becoming debilitating and provide a safe space to work through your emotions.

It comes as a lesson that our help comes from the Lord, He who is mighty enough to make Heaven and Earth. As you heal, you trust that you'll be able to survive the waves of emotional storms and be okay when you sit with them. Healing is not linear. Some days, you feel strong, and some days you crumble. Both are valid points. With our resilience reinforced and also allowing our vulnerability, you are building a sustainable road forward that respects all that makes us human as well as shows how you can adapt, survive, and gain meaning from this tragedy again.

Open and Empathic Toward Others

Experiencing loss makes us more attuned to the pain of others. We understand what it means to hurt deeply, and that understanding allows us to connect with others in profound ways. There is one thing we can attest to, that grief cracks us open. It is in this openness that you relearn, and you also expand to take on new heights of understanding. Active healing through empathy is putting the energy of one's pain into connection, rather than into isolation. It means giving the compassion you would've liked to have received, sitting with someone in their darkness without trying to fix it, and validating their experience. It means not holding onto pain, and not doing it because it was not done for you. When you extend compassion to others who are hurting, you confirm the fact that there is no need to be alone in suffering. Remember that grief is the universal price you pay for love, and that your presence for others honors that.

Willfully Purposed to Live Life

For many, grief becomes a catalyst for change. It inspires us to live more intentionally, to pursue what matters most, and to honor our loved ones through our actions. Loss pushes us to ask hard questions that are not often asked outside of life-changing circumstances: What matters? How do I want to spend my remaining time? What legacy do I want to leave?

After the initial impact of loss, many experience a shift in priorities. And as they navigate this new terrain, the superficial falls away, leaving a crystal-clear sense of what deserves our energy, versus what is a fleeting waste of time. Active healing through purpose means taking the lessons our loved ones taught us and weaving them into our routine. This is a way of paying homage while also processing and adapting to what it means to live on with their spirit as opposed to their physical presence. It's a stance against the bellows of grief, refusing to let it render our own lives meaningless. When we act with intention and make choices aligned with our deepest values, we engage in active healing. This increases consciousness, compassion, and courage.

Grief Requires Action: Helping Others Who Are Grieving

If you have taken away nothing else thus far, note that grief is a deeply personal journey, but no one should have to walk it alone. The struggle with helping others, or being a support to others who are grieved or grieving, is the desire to say or do the right thing. Supporting someone who is grieving requires patience, empathy, a removal of self, and a willingness to simply *be there.* I can recall the numerous times someone offered what they thought to be a supportive phrase. "They are in a better place now." or "Well, at least they are not in pain anymore." The intent of good completely missed the impact of hollow the phrase implied, leaving me feeling like I was wrong for wanting my loved one present. Often, the most helpful thing you can do is listen without trying to fix or explain—*just listen.* A small action goes a long way for a person who feels their entire world is scattered in pieces with no clear direction for collection.

Proactive social support is not merely comforting to those who are grieving. It also plays a vital role in preserving their mental and physical health.[21] People often put the responsibility on those who are grieving in an effort to respect their space and their decision. And while helpful, many times they add to the burden the person may already feel as "another thing to do." Therefore, be mindful, yet proactive. When considered as truly helpful, social support has been identified as one of the strongest predictors of positive outcomes following loss. Such a protective effect is not limited to the emotional well-being perspective.

21 Breen, L. J. (2021). "Harnessing Social Support for Bereavement Now and Beyond the COVID-19 Pandemic." *Palliat Care Soc Pract.* Feb 17, 2021.

Here are some ways to support others in their grief:

1. **Offer Presence, Not Answers**

   In a culture that often encourages moving on quickly and putting on a brave face, your willingness to sit with someone in their darkest moments offers a lifeline. You don't need perfect words or extraordinary gestures. It is through showing up, staying present, and demonstrating commitment through action that they don't have to carry this burden alone.

   - Avoid clichés like "everything happens for a reason" or "they're in a better place." Instead, say, "I'm here for you." Sit with them in their pain without trying to fill the silence.
   - Be understanding if their response when they are ready to speak is heavy or raw.
   - Be flexible, as they may want to talk about something unrelated to their loss and that is okay. Being present is the willingness to be flexible, and in being flexible, adapt when needed.

2. **Acknowledge Their Loss**

   Sometimes people avoid talking about the person who died, fearing they'll make the grieving person feel worse. But mentioning their loved one's name, sharing a memory, or simply saying, "I miss them too," can be incredibly comforting. It may seem small, but through my days, I just yearned for the permission to feel whatever I was feeling, and to know I was not in the way or going to have my feelings minimized or redirected. When you're with someone who's grieving:

   - Listen more than you talk. Resist the urge to fill silence with platitudes.
   - Accept all emotions without trying to fix them. Anger, guilt, relief, numbness—all are normal.
   - Avoid phrases that minimize pain: "At least they're not suffering" or "They're in a better place" may be well-intentioned but often feel dismissive.

- Use the deceased person's name. Don't avoid mentioning them out of fear of causing pain. The person you are speaking to is already thinking about them constantly. Show them, unless told otherwise, that you honor the space the person holds in their heart.
- Simple acknowledgments work best: "I can't imagine how painful this is," "Tell me about them," or simply, "I'm here." Your presence and willingness to witness their grief matters more than any words you might say.

3. **Provide Practical Support**

   Grief can make everyday tasks feel overwhelming. Offering to cook a meal, help with errands, or watch their kids can be a lifeline. Don't wait for the grieving person to ask for help. Make concrete offers instead of open-ended ones. Replace "Let me know if you need anything" with specific proposals:

   - "I'm going to the grocery store Tuesday. Can I pick up essentials for you?"
   - "I'd like to drop off dinner Thursday evening. Does 6:00 p.m. work?"
   - "I can watch the kids Saturday afternoon so you have time to yourself. Would that help?"
   - "I'm free to help with thank-you notes or funeral arrangements. Which would be most useful?"

The specificity removes the ambiguity, and an added item that seems unfinished or unattended to. The value of your willingness to step in and do the small things is immeasurable to the person's processing and navigation during this time.

1. **Check in Regularly**

   Grief doesn't follow a timeline, and support shouldn't either. The immediate blow of a death or loss often brings an outpouring of support. Cards arrive, meals are delivered, people gather. Then, within weeks, that support typically evaporates. In some cases, right when the grieving person needs it most. The acute shock begins wearing off, daily life resumes its demands, and the full weight of the loss settles in. Being a support does not mean you hold onto a rigid timeline of when and how you prodigy your support.

- Check in without the expectation that the person has to have a full conversation with you in return. All they may have is, "I am okay, thanks for checking in."
- Be okay with check-ins being physical. They may want to meet in the park and go for a walk to get fresh air, as opposed to just filtering calls and reminders that they have lost someone or something important.

2. **Know Your Capacity to Support**

   Supporting someone through grief requires emotional, spiritual, and mental energy. In unexpected moments, you may find yourself affected by their pain or exhausted by the weight of caregiving. This is an honest feeling and experience, this does not mean you're failing them or lacking adequate support for their situation. It means you're human, and that you cannot pour from an empty cup.

   - Set boundaries that allow you to sustain support over time.
   - Be mindful of your emotional and physical capacity.
   - Seek your own support when needed, whether through friends, your own counselor, or support groups for those caring for grieving individuals.
   - Taking care of yourself isn't selfish. It's what enables you to show up consistently for someone who needs you.

And most of all, Respect Their Journey.

Everyone grieves differently. Some may want to talk endlessly about their loss, while others may prefer solitude. Let them lead, and honor their way of coping. Being a part of the village, the community, is agreeing to provide the safety needed for it all to fall apart, not being allowed to dictate how it falls apart. I have learned that although people come to me for spiritual guidance, in grief, it is not always my place to guide. Rather, I accept the position of being a shoulder, or an open arm, because I gather in the moment what is more important, and that is to respect the journey and process that is grief.

> *"The friend who can be silent with us in a moment of despair or confusion, who can stay with us in an hour of grief and bereavement, who can tolerate not knowing … not healing, not curing … that is a friend who cares."*
>
> —Henri Nouwen

DISCUSSION QUESTIONS FOR STUDY GROUPS ON GRIEF

1. **How has grief shaped your understanding of God's love or your spiritual beliefs?**

   Reflect on whether your faith has grown, shifted, or been challenged through the process of grieving.

2. **What emotions in your grief feel most "unacceptable" to express to God, and what does that resistance reveal about your image of the divine?**

   Share moments when prayer or scripture helped you process overwhelming feelings.

3. **How do you interpret the promise in Psalm 34:18, "The Lord is nigh unto them that are of a broken heart; and saveth such as be of a contrite spirit."?**

   Discuss personal experiences of feeling God's presence—or absence—during grief.

4. **If your grief could speak a prayer, what would it say that your "composed self" is too afraid to articulate?**

   Explore how being part of a spiritual community has helped or hindered your journey.

5. **Has your loss made forgiveness harder or more urgent—and how does your faith navigate the tension between mercy and the right to rage?**

Consider whether new passions or callings have emerged from your grief.

6. **Which spiritual practices have become lifelines, and which have you abandoned because they now feel like empty practices?**

   Share how specific verses or practices have provided strength or hope.

7. **How do you balance holding onto the memories of your loved one while moving forward with your life?**

   Discuss how faith helps in integrating loss into a new sense of normalcy.

8. **What does "hope" look like for you in the midst of grief?**

   Reflect on how spiritual hope differs from simply "feeling better" and how it sustains you through pain.

9. **How do you navigate feelings of guilt when moments of joy or laughter arise after a significant loss?**

   Explore how faith or prayer can help in embracing joy without diminishing your grief.

10. **What has grief taught you about the limits of your own strength, and how has that humbling shaped your dependence on or distance from God?**

These questions are designed to open hearts and minds, encouraging honest conversations about the emotional and spiritual dimensions of grief.

ABOUT THE AUTHOR

For nearly four decades, Clive E. Neil has served as senior leader of Bedford Central Church in Brooklyn, New York, where his ministry has touched countless lives. A licensed psychotherapist specializing in human development, he brings deep insight into the challenges and transformation that shape our journeys.

Neil's academic foundation includes degrees from Eastern University, Princeton University, and Drew University, equipping him with both theological depth and psychological expertise. This unique combination informs his compassionate approach to faith and healing.

He is the author of *Dancing with Danger* and *Breaking Through*, works that reflect his commitment to helping readers navigate life's complexities with courage and grace. Through decades of pastoral care, counselling, and writing, Neil continues to guide individuals toward wholeness and hope.

ACKNOWLEDGMENTS

I am deeply grateful to the members and friends of Bedford Central Church, whose prayers, encouragement, and steadfast support have sustained me throughout this journey. I also extend my heartfelt appreciation to my biological family—especially my parents—whose love, sacrifice, and guidance laid the foundation for this work, and to my children Aisha and Darius for the insight and inspiration they gave me daily. I am profoundly thankful to my fiancée, Dr. Monica Joseph, for her patience, faith in me, and unwavering support. Special thanks to Shannon McLeod, whose careful editing, insight, and commitment helped shape this book into its final form. This work is richer because of each of you.

www.ingramcontent.com/pod-product-compliance
Lightning Source LLC
LaVergne TN
LVHW090958080826
845145LV00003B/1048

* 9 7 8 1 9 6 6 2 8 3 2 7 0 *